THE 20TH ANNIVERS

SILBURY DAWNING

THE *ALIEN VISITOR* GENE THEORY

JOHN COWIE

First published in Great Britain by The Media Shack in 2000

The 20th Anniversary Edition includes all information from the previous three editions.

© John Cowie 2000, 2002, 2012, 2020
This book is copyright under the Berne Convention.

ISBN: 979 862152 62 83

0 1 6 2 0 9 6 5 7

A CIP catalogue record for this book is available from the British Library

www.silburydawning.com

With special thanks to my daughter Felicity whose editing skills and collaboration made this book possible.

'The Universe will sort things out.'

John Cowie

CONTENTS

FOREWORD TO THE 20ᵀᴴ ANNIVERSARY EDITION

As the author of a book about aliens and pyramids I have been, unsurprisingly, frequently asked during the 20 years since publication 'where do you get your ideas from'.

The purpose of the book is to answer that question and argues that the unexplained 'missing link', or rapid jump in our human evolution, was conditioned by a visiting alien technology.

More personally, I've come to understand, in the last two decades, that the passion and conviction which generated my book has much to do with a rather unique set of life circumstances.

Although I started writing the book in 1996, the ideas for it began with my working life selling sand, incredibly transformed into the world-changing 'silicon chip' at the start of our Technological Revolution, as we are starting to call the times in which we are living.

Aged 29, I started working in the silicon chip industry in 1974 and found myself in a world which took my breath away. How was everything developing so fast? And the idea started to grow in me that perhaps this speed of innovation wasn't just about pure *discovery* but rather conditioned by a *recovery* of things we already knew.

In the early 1980s I moved from Scotland to work at Intel's UK headquarters in Wiltshire, England. My job involved a helping Intel sell their semiconductors and rapidly developing microprocessors around the world. Often on the road, I frequently passed a local landmark called Silbury Hill, not as well-known internationally as Stonehenge or Avebury (also in Wiltshire) but similarly credited as an ancient construction, purpose unknown.

Alongside all this, my father had urged me to read Erich von Däniken's *Chariots of the Gods: Unsolved Mysteries of the Past* which argues that the gods we credit with shaping our earliest cultures and technologies were actually alien astronauts.

I feel it was out of these circumstances I started to write the book in 1996, shortly after my father's death.

From the outset, the book was self-published and had its own website. I was also one of the early adopters of selling a book online. I think I took this decision instinctively because I was fascinated by the possibilities offered by directly interacting with readers. I also wanted to get my book out as soon as possible. It was always a book for sharing.

My instincts were right and because of this approach *Silbury Dawning* is what I think of as a 'living book'.

In the last two decades I've come to discover, through reactions to my book, just how many of us give a great deal of thought to the question 'where do we come from'. To date, the website has attracted more than a million registered users, many of whom have engaged in forums. I've sold more than 6,000 hard and digital copies to people all around the world and hundreds of copies of a spin-off poster about Silbury Hill. But beyond those figures, the book has given me the access to connect with many other thinkers and the book has been frequently updated with their ideas.

In fact, a whole new chapter (Pyramids, Chapter 6) sprang out of various wonderful opportunities.

In this 20th anniversary edition I've included a Timeline of the book so that it's possible to follow the book's life and the way in which it has attracted opportunities and ideas. The Timeline is followed by additional material generated by that engagement.

I have heard people start to describe the coming phase of our Technological Revolution as the Age of Artificial Intelligence and, in early 2020, this is something which is met with both hope and trepidation.

I feel that my book shows our thirst for innovation or what I've come to think of as *recovery* of knowledge. The more we realise is hidden, the more we desire to get to the truth. My hope is that my book will give us confidence that despite the challenges that lie ahead we do have solutions. Tantalisingly, perhaps we ourselves are a form of artificial intelligence in which an earlier and superior technology is embedded. I believe our thirst for knowledge comes from a deeper understanding that we can empower ourselves with that technology.

John Cowie

INTRODUCTION

This book will try to explain how we have evolved from ape-like creatures into a race that has the intelligence and skills to perform heart transplants, convert sand into computers, communicate via satellites and put a man on the moon.

Why do human beings possess intelligence so superior to that of their closest relatives, especially when it is known that they share 98.4 per cent of their genetic make-up with the African chimpanzee?

Many theories of evolution centre on the idea it is a struggle for survival that forces the development of early life-forms into complex beings. But this fails to explain the evolution of functions of the human brain which seem unconnected with survival. These functions include understanding irony, creating complicated mathematical formulae, writing poetry or even designing striped toothpaste.

I find it difficult to accept that our intelligence is purely the result of the slow process of evolution. After all, it took around two million years for our earliest ancestors to appear. But in just a hundred years we have seen the average IQ, height, longevity of life of our race increase demonstrably. And in the past 30 years, I have witnessed phenomenal developments in the computer and communication industries in which I have worked all my life.

It seems to me that at some point along our evolutionary path we may have had some help which enabled us to make our outstanding achievements.

My theory is that the rapid evolution of our intelligence is due to the arrival on Earth of a highly intelligent extra-terrestrial being, or race of beings – which I will call the *Alien Visitor* throughout this book – that bred with, or somehow planted its genetic material and educated our *Homo sapiens* ancestors.

I believe the arrival of the *Alien Visitor* advanced our evolution by millions of years. Without this, we could still be slowly travelling along the evolutionary timeline, developing our intelligence as we struggle to survive. Our skills today would probably be similar to those our ancestors held in the Dark Ages. Or worse, we could be extinct along with many other species of ape.

I want to explore the idea that we all possess this extra-terrestrial intelligence, which we inherited from the *Alien Visitor*.

Chapter 1

DAWNING

I first became interested in the idea of the arrival of an *Alien Visitor* on Earth owing to my fascination with Silbury Hill[1] which is located near my home in Wiltshire.

In my excursions to and from work, I have seen Silbury Hill in many different colours and moods. In a playful mood the mound is light green and someone flies a kite from the top but on a journey home at night it stands alone and ancient. There are times, particularly against the backdrop of the sun rising or setting in the sky, with a mist clinging to the surrounding terrain, that I have been drawn to stand and gaze and wonder. On moments like these there is a dawning in me that something especially significant to our remarkable development took place here a long, long time ago. It seems to me that Silbury Hill is a witness to the evolution of man and perhaps holds answers to the mysteries of our origins that confound us.

It is the largest man-made mound in Europe and thought to be around 4,500 years old. But its function and the reason why it was built remain a mystery to this day. Digs have searched for treasure and burial chambers but nothing has ever been found. I started to think that perhaps the key to the hill's function could be found by

---

[1] Silbury Hill has survived even Roman road construction and stands close to the A4 between Calne and Marlborough, near the Beckhampton roundabout in Wiltshire, England.

looking at its shape and location, rather than by excavation. Today we see Silbury Hill as a grass mound, but it was originally built from large blocks of locally quarried chalk. Some archaeologists suggest that it might be of similar age and construction to the ancient Egyptian stepped pyramid at Saqqarah and the pyramid of Cuicuilco in Mexico.

Silbury Hill is surrounded by similar constructions whose original functions are also unknown. I think they may have been part of a very large complex which I believe could have been more extensive than we imagine. They include the stone circles at Avebury and the megaliths at Stonehenge. What fascinates me about these sites is trying to imagine what they originally looked like – cut into the lush vegetation and forests that have long since disappeared. Many of the stones are missing and some may have been re-arranged. I wonder what the original shapes of these bluestones were before they became weathered and tourists chipped away their own souvenirs. What also remains is evidence of deep ditches, banks and round barrows or tumuli that encircle the stone structures. It is possible these grassy banks may have originally been white rings of limestone which could make the site more conspicuous and perhaps easier to find, either from the ground or the sky. We do not know which conclusions could be derived from the shadows cast by the stones on these concentric white circles and white barrows. It is uncertain what information these structures provided at the various times of the day and different days of the year or whether they were meant to be viewed from the ground or from above. As with Silbury Hill, we can only guess at the functions of these constructions, but they all point to a mass of people prepared to work very hard in relative harmony, who were ordered by an architect or group of architects who designed the sites. Is the real significance of these sites that they were designed and built by someone who was able to look down on our landscape?

The fields that surround Silbury Hill are a popular site for crop circles. A number of these fantastically designed formations in the crops have been dismissed as the work of hoaxers. Others have prompted researchers from all over the world to take a closer look. Like Silbury Hill, these circles are an enigma. I began to wonder if perhaps this was further evidence that the hill could be some kind of beacon, which can be viewed from high in the sky.

Maybe it has attracted the landings of spacecraft, which many believe are responsible for the crop circles. It occurred to me that if this were the true explanation for the construction of Silbury Hill then it might have been used as a beacon for thousands of years. Perhaps it was built for the purpose of attracting craft to a safe landing site. It was a fantastic idea but one, which I could not shake off, especially with its close proximity to Stonehenge and the stone circles at Avebury. All of these structures share similar features. The purpose of their construction is unclear. It is not known how the large stones – which are not from the area – could have been moved into place or how a large hill could have been built by hand. All the sites are visible from the sky. These mysterious structures are not just found in the West of England but across the world. There are the pyramids in Egypt, Yucatan and the Canary Islands and a similar construction to Stonehenge in China to name just a few.

In Britain at the time when Silbury Hill, the megaliths at Stonehenge and the stone circles at Avebury were built, societies did not seem to be very developed – especially not advanced enough to have designed aircraft.

Hunters, fishermen and farmers dominated these societies. The demands of coping with the violence of nature are likely to have shaped the rituals of daily life. It seems remarkable that these people would have needed or wanted to build a beacon for aircraft. I believe the *Alien Visitor* came to our planet at some point between the emergence of our early ancestors and the building of these complex structures. For this reason, I feel certain all these structures could turn out to be even older than the generally accepted theory and all built within the *Alien Visitor* age. The *Alien Visitor* was highly intelligent, an assumption made owing to its ability to find and land on our planet. It was able to adapt to the conditions on Earth and use the resources it encountered to survive.

The *Alien Visitor* left behind clues to confirm its visit to our planet. Several can be found in the physical evidence that exists on Earth and other clues can be found in the functions of our developed brains.

Chapter 2

THE BIG PICTURE

We are starting to learn how Earth was created and how life on the planet began when boiling water reacted with chemicals creating simple creatures. In turn, these simple creatures reproduced and evolved into more complex animals and plants. If it happened on Earth, it is highly probable it could have all happened on another planet many, many years before.

Many scientists are convinced that life on other planets is a possibility because of the resilience of some kinds of bacteria that can tolerate extraordinary conditions on Earth.

I believe the highest life-form on another planet could have found a way of arriving and surviving on Earth and changing the gradual evolution process for our ancestors, developing them from apes into intelligent human beings.

Our solar system began forming many billions of years ago from a huge cloud of interstellar gas, dust and debris left over from the birth of the Sun. The Earth then built up over millions of years as its gravitational pull attracted material from the cloud. Analysis of tiny fragments of lunar rock has revealed that the moon appears to have been formed from the debris of a collision between Earth and an object bigger than Mars some 50 million years after the start of the solar system. Similar events continue to occur throughout the galaxy.

As life requires water then water must be a pre-requisite for the beginning of life itself. The reaction of the cooling of Earth's crust against the cold windowpane of space produced boiling steam and subsequently water. Our atmosphere, which was initially composed mainly of methane and ammonia, slowly broke down into nitrogen, hydrogen and carbon dioxide. The lightweight hydrogen then escaped into space leaving nitrogen and carbon dioxide. Soon, water vapour in the upper atmosphere was broken down into hydrogen and oxygen. The hydrogen escaped into space, but the oxygen stayed and soon formed an ozone layer. After the formation of the atmosphere, the simple chemicals that are very common in space were transformed into larger molecules. These first primitive molecules, known as protocells, were created. Scientists at the NASA Ames Research Centre and the University of California, Santa Cruz, believe that protocells are critical for the origin of life.

Blue-green algae then began to form on or near the surface of the Earth's oceans. They converted the planet's supply of carbon dioxide into oxygen. Soon plants began to grow on land and the oxygen and carbon dioxide levels began to balance. The genetic study of fossil plant spores that date back 500 million years reveals that land plants arose as a single natural group when puddles of green algae evolved into liverworts.

If this can happen on Earth, then it is more than likely to have happened elsewhere. In fact, we have discovered that Mars once supported liquid water and the moon has around six billion metric tons of water contained in the soil – most of it at the South Pole of the moon. If we can confirm a number of planets that support or supported liquid water in our solar system, then this dramatically increases the odds for water-bearing planets and hence the chance of life evolving in many other galaxies in the universe.

We know hydrogen and oxygen bond to form ice, in possibly 15 different ways on Earth and do exactly the same on the Moon, Mars and on Jupiter's moons Europa and Callisto. Carbon atoms behave in the same way elsewhere in the universe. Given the right conditions of pressure and temperature they will bond with other atoms into patterns, forming graphite or diamonds. Spectrometry has shown that the universe is made up of the same elements and gases but in differing proportions of course. Debris from an exploding star – which is known as iron-60 – and a sprinkling of dust from a comet have gone some way to confirming the idea that the same elements exist in other parts of space. This helps us expand our understanding of our solar system. Mars is much more like Earth than was previously thought, according to the first official results of the Mars Pathfinder mission which landed on the red planet in 1997. An analysis of the wealth of data the mission sent back has shown that Martian geology appears to be perhaps as varied and elaborate as Earth's, which means that the planet was more active in its past. There is evidence of abundant water in the past and it has an iron core similar to Earth's. Rocks on Mars have low magnesium concentration but are rich in silicon, aluminium and potassium. This is similar to rocks on Earth's crust. Some have suggested that Mars and the Earth might once have been a single planet, which broke into two parts, with the Moon being separated as a droplet of material between them. I think the *Alien Visitor* could have been the life-form of another planet which was created in the same way as Earth but many aeons before.

It has been mathematically established that the likelihood of other forms of alien life in the universe is highly probable. Huge strides have been made in the hunt for alien life. Astronomers from the Search for Extra-Terrestrial Intelligence (SETI) Institute in America, which works with NASA and Britain's Jodrell Bank observatory, have found evidence of another solar system with Earth-size planets potentially able to support life. The launch of NASA's Kepler observatory in 2009 has been very significant. In three years, Kepler has discovered 61 new confirmed planets and uncovered the possible existence of 2,300 more. Some potential Earth-like candidates include CoRoT-7b a rocky planet just 4.8 times the mass of Earth, and Gliese 581c the most earth-like planet found so far, five times as massive as Earth and possibly bearing liquid water.

Some physicists believe that all the essential amino acids needed for life on Earth have been identified in meteorites. As these comets and meteorites came from elsewhere in the universe it seems possible that there are other planets made up of the same amino acids as Earth. This could indicate the possibility of life in other parts of the universe. By exploring this possibility, could we be the first generation on Earth to discover alien life?

When the *Alien Visitor* arrived on Earth it would have been able to use its immense mathematical, scientific and technological knowledge to survive because the universe shares the same elements, atoms, weather patterns and scientific laws. For example, in our solar system there are three planets with similar gravitational field strengths to our own – Venus, which is of similar mass and diameter; Saturn's mass is 95 times more and its diameter nine times bigger; and Uranus's mass is 15 times more and its diameter four times bigger. The *Alien Visitor* will have calculated that Earth's gravity was not that different from its own planet and may have also discerned that the troposphere – the layer of atmosphere closest to the Earth (21 per cent oxygen and 78 per cent nitrogen) – was a suitable environment in which it could survive. Of course, there is no way of knowing whether the *Alien Visitor's* arrival on Earth had been planned for many years and followed meticulous calculations or whether the decision to land was taken in a split second as the visitor's craft plummeted towards Earth.

However, in the vastness of our galaxy, with the many obstacles in space from meteorites to black holes to gamma ray bursts unleashing devastating amounts of radiation in seconds, how could an alien life-form travel from one planet to another? On Earth, we have so far only managed to send people as far as the moon, although this is not just due to the dangers in space but the human body's own difficulty in travelling outside our own atmosphere. Perhaps the *Alien Visitor* had discovered how to travel faster than the speed of light, or maybe it used a shortcut to travel through anomalies in space, such as a 'wormhole' which Albert Einstein thought may have existed, connecting link points in space separated by billions of miles. They are best explained by drawing two spots on a piece of paper and bending the paper so that the point where the two dots touch is very small. The spots come together but remain the same distance apart on the paper. Or did the *Alien Visitor* find a way to harness the 'plankton' of energy particles in space to propel its spacecraft?

Another possibility is that the *Alien Visitor's* home planet had a much longer elliptical path around its sun than Earth and at a point some 13,000 years ago its trajectory came closest to Earth's orbit, close enough for the *Alien Visitor's* to travel in a space vehicle and land on Earth. If this were possible at that stage in the cycle then there may be other times when the *Alien Visitor* could reach our planet. What is the current position of the *Alien Visitor's* planet on its orbit relative to Earth – and will it return?

Chapter 3

THE BIRTH OF THE HUMAN RACE

I think it is possible to suggest a large but narrowing window in time when the *Alien Visitor* would have landed on Earth. Our first ancestors – which can be traced back from modern man – appeared over two million years ago. They were a family called *Homo* made up of a number of different species. Those that survived the Ice Age – which ended around 18,000 years ago, according to evidence held in ice cores and sediments – had developed skills to hunt animals much bigger and stronger than themselves, butcher their kill, live in shelters usually at the mouths of caves and work as a community. I believe that the *Alien Visitor* arrived sometime after this Ice Age. These *Homo* species had developed into the first pharaohs to rule Egypt some 7,000 years ago. By this time, the *Alien Visitor* had long gone.

I presuppose the *Alien Visitor* arrived in this period because it was a time of rapid development of our ancestors, especially when put in the context of the two million years it took for our earliest ancestors to first appear on Earth. If we take a look at our very gradual evolution before the arrival of the *Alien Visitor*, we can chart a period where the development of life was advanced or hampered by a multitude of changes and coincidences. I think it is impossible for this same hit-or-miss process to have brought about the unusual leap in our evolution from *Homo* to pharaoh.

These dates can only be gauged by our current discoveries of the remains of early man and the early civilisations. Our evolution is recognised as one of the most controversial areas of science with many questions still unanswered. Further discoveries may reveal new evidence to show exactly how, when and where this first advanced civilisation began. In addition, we may also find our radiocarbon dating techniques imprecise and replace them with others, which also date these civilisations to earlier times. In this case I would argue that the *Alien Visitor* came earlier, for it is this visitor which gave early man the ability to create these civilisations.

I believe this highly intelligent extra-terrestrial life-form bred with, or somehow implanted its genetic material and educated our *Homo* ancestors, thus speeding up our development. This may seem a fantastic suggestion, but as BBC presenter Peter Allen suggested in his comments on this book:

"Since mankind is clearly going to have the capacity to plant its genetic structure around the universe within the next few hundred years - it seems logical that we are ourselves the product of such a process".

I think the *Alien Visitor* took a special interest in our ancestors because they were strong and receptive to the *Alien Visitor's* demands. They would have made good 'workhorses'. We can obviously never really know why the *Alien Visitor* decided to mate with or somehow implant its genetic material in our ancestors instead of other animals, but I can put forward a few suggestions.

Perhaps early man already had functions – such as fingers and opposable thumbs – which enabled him to carry out tasks quickly. Maybe the *Alien Visitor* needed to use a race that had height, strength and speed. We can never know if the *Alien Visitor* looked like us or reproduced in the same way as humans or in fact if there was any rational thought behind the *Alien Visitor's* decision to use our ancestors. Maybe the *Alien Visitor* was simply and inexplicably attracted to them. There is no way of knowing how the gene was dispersed but I do believe it became present in our male and female ancestors and soon became very widespread. It is also impossible to be certain if this gene created different races or if these varieties of our early ancestors already existed before the arrival of the *Alien Visitor*.

We have evidence of the build of early *Homo* species that lived on the planet just before the period in which I believe the *Alien Visitor* arrived. Scientists discovered a fossil footprint trail on the shores of the Langebaan Lagoon, a beauty spot on the Atlantic coast 60 miles north of Cape Town. They believe the footprints were made by a *Homo neanderthalensis* female who lived around 117,000 years ago but had some similar characteristics to modern woman. These include walking upright with a jutting jaw and having a high forehead. Scientists named her Genetic Eve[2] and perhaps, by the time the *Alien Visitor* had arrived, this strong and tall, or at least upright build, was suited to the manual work the *Alien Visitor* needed to be carried out on the planet. The BBC human documentary series *Ape-Man*[3] explores how

---

[2] Named by Dr Lee Berger, a paleo-anthropologist at the University of the Witwatersrand in Johannesburg.

[3] Human documentary series that explores the origins of mankind *Ape-Man*. First shown on BBC2

Genetic Eve and her descendants had migrated in search of more dependable sources of shellfish and fish along the coastline and riverbanks in order to support their steadily increasing population. This documentary provides evidence to show that during the next 100,000 years, Genetic Eve had slowly progressed along the coastline south through Southern Asia and Australia and north following rivers like the Nile to Egypt, the Middle East and Europe. The programme also explains how the species *Homo heidelbergensis* had thrived in the colder areas of Europe and through necessity had made the transition from scavenger to hunter. So these early ancestors were very mobile and resilient, prior to the arrival of the *Alien Visitor*.

By the time the *Alien Visitor* had arrived, our *Homo* ancestors had interbred and evolved into a fully upright, bipedal animal with similar skull size to modern humans and had proliferated into many parts of the world. They were capable of shaping utensils and arrowheads, creating body decoration and ornaments and were also burying their dead. They also practised division of labour between the sexes and food sharing. The muscular physique of these early people and their ability to use tools may explain why the *Alien Visitor* wanted to use them, rather than other animals, for work.

Perhaps, more than any other strong animal, they understood and were able to respond to the commands of the *Alien Visitor*. Anthropologists from Duke University Medical Centre in North Carolina say they have anatomical evidence that suggests that the *Neanderthals* – which predated *Homo sapiens* – may have had vocal

February 2000.

abilities, which means they could be capable of communication with sounds. Maybe the *Alien Visitor* chose to work with the *Homo* species because they were able to share some kind of verbal communications and perhaps this became more developed as time passed, so that the *Homo* species rapidly developed their sounds into a kind of language which they shared with the *Alien Visitor*.

Perhaps, what started as a master and slave relationship developed and the *Alien Visitor* started to pass on its ideas and knowledge to the *Homo* species? Maybe the hominids, with the capacity for speech and art, were quick to learn and fascinated by this visitor. I think they may have been like sponges for the information the *Alien Visitor* had to impart.

The relationship between the *Alien Visitor* and the *Homo* species may have been like that between Prospero and Caliban in *The Tempest*[4]. Prospero initially uses Caliban as a workhorse:

PROSPERO He does make our fire, fetch in our wood, and serves in offices that profit us. What, ho! Slave! Caliban.

But later Prospero takes a greater interest in Caliban and allows him to live with him in his "cell" and passes on his learning, which Caliban acknowledges:

CALIBAN You taught me language.

Once the *Alien Visitor* gene had been introduced to the slowly evolving *Homo* species, the race started to develop very quickly and was rapidly distinguished from other related species. I believe the introduction of this

---

[4] William Shakespeare *The Tempest* Routledge 1988

alien gene explains why such a young species of *Homo,* which we define as *Homo sapiens,* separated and evolved so quickly into what we eventually call the human race and looks so different from related species.

Just how different we look from our closest relatives in the animal world would become clear if we were to try to take our place in a 'police-style' identity parade made up of the one hundred and ninety-two living species of monkeys and apes. Even if we stood at one end of the row next to the tailless great apes and nearest relatives such as the chimpanzee, bonobo and gorilla, we would still look out of place. Our legs are too long, arms too short and our feet seem rather strange. If the members of the parade were led out, it would be clear that we walk differently.

The other obvious and rather dramatic difference is, except for conspicuous tufts of hair on the head, in the armpits and around the genitals, the skin surface is completely exposed. Why did we not maintain a coat, similar to our closest relatives, to protect us from the harmful rays of the sun or the varying temperatures? Zoologically, it does not make sense that the human being, in particular the human female, is almost completely devoid of hair. Unfortunately, fossils cannot help us when it comes to differences in skin and hair, so we have no idea as to exactly when we lost our hair. Many theories have been put forward to explain why our skin is fully exposed to the outside world. One idea is that the human exposed himself to a much greater range of temperatures than he had previously experienced when he left forests for open plains and he lost his coat to prevent himself from becoming overheated. Another theory is by losing hair and by increasing the number of sweat glands all over the body surface, cooling could be achieved. But this still does not explain why none of the other primates and carnivores lost its coat. Another puzzling difference is our unique slimy lips. Anatomists have stated that their evolution is not yet clearly understood. Perhaps it is these differences which made our ancestors attractive to the *Alien Visitor* because maybe they had them in common. Or perhaps these were physical traits of the *Alien Visitor,* which were passed onto our ancestors along with intelligence. Maybe the *Alien Visitor* selected our ancestors for reproduction because they looked the most similar to the visitor out of all the creatures on Earth. Could it be that the human form had already evolved on the alien planet as the best design for the pursuit of intelligent activity, which was starting to take shape on Earth? Perhaps the human body is the best design for intelligent life in the universe. It would be nice to think so. The only animal, which we believe comes close to our level on intelligence, is the dolphin. Scientists have found we share similar genes. However, dolphins are perhaps not able to exploit their intelligence because they are compelled to live in water which restricts them from the activity's humans are fit to explore.

We can piece together research gained from fossils to see how the human evolved. At the beginning, according to scientific research carried out at Bristol University and Washington University in Seattle, man's ultimate ancestor was a pig-like creature that lived 250 million years ago in a South African desert. Scientists believe this was Earth's first warm-blooded being and man's earliest known ancestor. They believe the *lystrosaur* links the earliest vertebrate life-forms, which crawled out of the sea onto land, to man. The *lystrosaur* survived and evolved into a rodent, progressing over a long period into apes and then man. Their resilience is attributed to the flexibility of a fleshy snout that allowed them to eat plants growing in crevices where other animals, including their predators, could not reach. Palaeontologists have found that the *lystrosaur*, a pre-Jurassic pig, survived an unknown natural disaster, which led to the extinction of many life-forms. The disaster remains a mystery, but theories include volcanic activity, tectonic movement, an influx of interplanetary dust, or an asteroid strike which raised temperatures to an estimated 60° C.

Footprints and fossils baked into rock in the remote Karoo area of South Africa have given scientists a picture of the pig. Using sophisticated electronic scanning equipment, designed for brain surgery, scientists discovered that the *lystrosaur* had a series of very thin bones called turbinate's in its nasal passages, which were designed to warm air as it was inhaled. This indicates that the creature was warm-blooded which is a vital prerequisite for the development of higher brain function.

The ape first appears some 15 million years ago. The apes that made the first steps on the human journey are called australopithecines. Small, vulnerable mammals, their safety probably rested in numbers and their ability to escape into trees if danger threatened. The ability to walk upright was first seen more than four million years ago in the australopithecine species, *Australopithecus anamensis*. At some ambiguous point about two million years ago, they became sufficiently different from the first upright apes to deserve a new name. From then on, we recognise them as close family and call them *Homo*. Scientists still do not know exactly which one of the australopithecine led to the first *Homo* species. The *Homo* family, like the australopithecine, divides into various branches which eventually produce *Homo sapiens*. The definition of *Homo sapiens* is changing as we learn more about our ancestors and how they differ from other species. It is a category that includes the now extinct primitive man and modern man. In recent years the remains of *Homo sapiens* have been classified as such because they have a large cranial capacity, opposable thumbs and forefingers and the ability to make stone tools. Other species, which were once considered human, have been reassigned to a non-human hominid category because they do not share these characteristics. A skull of one of the early hominids called *Australopithecus africanus* who lived some 2.6 to 2.8 million years ago is estimated to have had a brain capacity of about 515 cubic centimetres, similar to that of a modern chimpanzee. Increased cranial capacity has been found in *Homo habilis* from about two million years ago. He had a cranial capacity of more than 600 cubic centimetres. A later species, *Homo ergaster*, which evolved in Africa, possibly from *Homo habilis*, had a cranial capacity of 800 to 1,100 cubic centimetres. Today the average human brain is about 1,350 cubic centimetres. The largest brain on record is 2,500 cubic centimetres. In this context, it seems the brain grew very rapidly even though the evolution of pig to *Homo sapiens* took a very long time. I believe this points to a catalyst in our development which I am convinced was the *Alien Visitor*.

After the *Alien Visitor* had left the planet, *Homo sapiens* continued to evolve rapidly because of the *Alien Visitor* gene which gave the species many advantages not enjoyed by other animals. This theory of competition is explained by Charles Darwin:

Natural selection acts solely through the preservation of variations in some way advantageous, which consequently endure. But as from the high geometrical powers of increase of all organic beings, each area is already fully stocked with inhabitants, it follows that as each selected and favoured forms increases in number, so will the less favoured forms decrease and become rare. Rarity as geology tells us, is a precursor to extinction.[5]

I think *Homo sapiens,* which did not gain this *Alien Visitor* gene struggled to compete against their counterparts and reduced in number. Creatures such as the Yeti or Big Foot – which some academics believe survive in the wildernesses of the former Soviet Union and North America – could be the remaining members of this side-lined race. Perhaps they are examples of what human beings would be like today if the *Alien Visitor* had not altered the course of our evolution.

Even with just one *Alien Visitor*, the gene could be rapidly spread in the future *Homo sapiens* generations. Mathematically we can see how multiplication is a powerful engine for growth – even with an insignificantly low number like two (if we assume that there was only one *Alien Visitor*). There is an old tale about the mathematician who invented the game of chess that illustrates this very well. The king liked the game so much, the story goes, that he offered the mathematician any prize. The mathematician asked only for two grains of wheat to be placed on the first square of the chessboard, four on the second, eight on the third and so

---

[5] Charles Darwin *The Origin of Species* Penguin 1985

forth, doubling the number of grains of wheat for each of the sixty-four squares on the chessboard. The story says that in the end he gained more grain than the number of human beings that have existed in the entire history of the world.

The proof of the advantage of this strong gene is that although most other animal families are made up of many species, this is known as adaptive radiation, the human only has one member – the *Homo sapiens*. This suggests that our population started from a single point and successfully prevented any competition. I think there were a number of species of bipedal hominids that had gained the *Alien Visitor* Gene. To complicate matters further, it is also likely that those early humans as defined as having the *Alien Visitor* gene may have continued to breed with other *Homo* species without the extra-terrestrial DNA including Neanderthals? Those species with larger skulls and hence bigger brains were successful. I believe this explains why scientists analysing the genetic blueprint for humans have found that 99.99 per cent of this code is the same for everyone. They also discovered that where there are differences, they do not result in different ethnic groups. That is to say, research showed that people from different ethnic groups can have more in common, genetically, than those from the same group. Some scientists refer to the theory that the human race started from a single point as the Replacement Theory, also known as the Out of Africa model.

[6]Professor Stephen Oppenheimer's research based on a synthesis of the mtDNA and Y chromosome

---

[6] Professor Stephen Oppenheimer, Oxford University is author of the books *"The Origins of the*

evidence with archaeology, climatology, fossil study and other data, track the migration routes and interaction of our ancient ancestors over the last 160,000 years. Although there is no suggestion of an *Alien Visitor* gene in his investigations, what I find very interesting about his research is his submission that something significant to our human evolution occurred somewhere between 15,000 and 7,500 years ago after the melting of the ice caps but before the land broke away from the mainland and divide into islands. The date I suggest from my research for the arrival of an *Alien Visitor* of approximately 13,000 years ago fits neatly into this window.

"We are all born with an extraordinary interest in where we came from and who our relatives are", says Professor Oppenheimer. "This really brings home that we are just one big, very close family."

The startling result of the new picture of human evolution of just how very closely related all humans are confirms the supposition that modern genetics has now shown that the 'Out of Africa' theory may be correct and confirms my theory that our population started from a single point and successfully prevented any competition.

The essence of the theory is that we all descend from a group of people who lived in Africa, then spread out across the world, replacing the local hominids everywhere else. For the same reasons as the original *Alien Visitor*, the hybrid *Alien Visitor* and *Homo sapiens* chose to breed with other *Homo sapiens*. We cannot be sure what these reasons are. As a result of this, the other hominid groups died out because they did not receive the

---

British: A Genetic Detective Story" and "Out of Eden: The Peopling of the World".

Alien Visitor gene and could not compete with the hybrids. I am in no doubt that the arrival of the *Alien Visitor* – and the dispersal of its subsequent offspring across the world – replaced all of our nearest ancestors. But as I believe the *Alien Visitor's* base was in Egypt, I hypothesise the human race originated there, rather than South Africa. Incidentally, I think the *Homo sapiens* may have developed different features because they lived in different climates – for example, some may have darker or lighter skin. This difference of appearance may not have mattered to the *Alien Visitor* because the *Homo sapiens* as a species shared features which were useful or attractive to the *Alien Visitor*. I believe these differences in appearance explain why humans today can look so different. It is also entirely possible that there may have been more than one *Alien Visitor* and although they were of the same species they may have looked different from each other. It may also be possible that there were more than one species of *Alien Visitor*!

We know that in this period, when the *Alien Visitor* arrived and thrived on Earth, many creatures became extinct. Maybe this is because the *Alien Visitor* brought new diseases to the planet or started to eat, use and make goods out of the animals, altering the food chain. Perhaps it may confirm that these animals were destroyed by some global catastrophe that could also explain the disappearance of the *Alien Visitor*. Examinations of the remains of the largest mammals that became extinct some 10,000 years ago may shed some light on their sudden demise. If they died of a disease, it may still exist, waiting to be awakened as we come across the remains of these creatures. Some have already been found under the Siberian permafrost.

So far I have argued for when the *Alien Visitor* arrived and the impact it had on our evolution. But I believe that this rapid development of man is not only due to the *Alien Visitor* gene but also due to the cultural influence of the *Alien Visitor* on primitive man.

Chapter 4

CIVILISATION

What caused our *Homo sapiens* ancestors to move from small nomadic family groups into large settlements? Did fear for their safety from other groups drive them into larger assemblies, or did they develop different skills from their neighbours that led to bartering which slowly developed into a widespread trading network? These conventional theories for the birth of the early cities and civilisations such as Caral in Peru ignore one critical factor – a universal knowledge. Where did these first civilisations, that share similar features, obtain this universal knowledge? For example pyramids employing complex mathematical techniques appear in early civilisations across the world!

I firmly believe that the *Alien Visitor* was the founder of our earliest civilisations and that around 13,000 years ago, there was a much higher level of knowledge on our planet which we are slowly reclaiming today.

We have established a time when the *Alien Visitor* landed but we need to explore where it might have landed. I suggest that it landed in Egypt and formed a civilisation around 7,000 – 8,000 years earlier than the recognised civilisation of 5000 BC. Recent archaeological research suggests that parts of this second civilisation are much older. Many Egyptologists are beginning to suggest that score marks and the erosion on the Sphinx could have been caused by heavy rainfall. But the heavy rains stopped falling in this area around 7,000 years ago. This suggests that the Sphinx was built earlier when rainfall was common. In his book *Sacred Science*[7], Schwaller de Lubicz argues that the body of the Sphinx shows indisputable signs of erosion due to rainfall. In addition to this, fossils of shells have been found around the base of the Pyramids and boats have been found buried near the Pyramids. The wear and tear marks on these 143 ft-long boats show they sailed on the water many times. Finally, earlier this century, the mystic and philosopher, George Ivanovich Gurdjieff found a map of Egypt that showed it to be devoid of any sand, showing the country was once subject to rain.

If we accept that the Sphinx and pyramids complex were built around 7,000 years earlier than the recognised civilisation of 5000 BC, it can be argued that the *Alien Visitor* – who had landed on the planet – built and ordered this civilisation. I am not arguing that the famous civilisation of 5000 BC happened earlier because I concur this did take place in 5000 BC but I think it was the second civilisation to spring up in Egypt and encompassed the site of the earlier *Alien Visitor* civilisation.

The construction of Silbury Hill has been likened to that of the Egyptian pyramids, particularly King Djoser's step pyramid at Saqqara and has also been dated at a similar period. But if as I have argued, the Egyptian pyramids were built at least 7,000 years earlier than the

---

[7] R.A. Schwaller de Lubicz *Sacred Science* Inner Traditions International 1988

time in which archaeologists currently believe they were built, then Silbury Hill could also be a much older structure. This would also apply to the structures at Stonehenge and Avebury which archaeologists concur as being built in the more recent Neolithic times. It is possible that Silbury Hill, along with the other pyramids in Yucatan, Mexico and the Canary Islands may have all been linked to the central Egyptian pyramid complex in Giza. This suggests that the *Alien Visitor* had also established many settlements across the temperate climate belt at this time. In a Channel Four documentary, *Quest For The Lost Civilisation*[8], Graham Hancock argues that these pyramids are part of a worldwide network.

I do not know why the *Alien Visitor* chose to come to our planet, why Egypt was selected as a landing place and why a network of pyramids was constructed. Could it be that quite simply, the *Alien Visitor* found itself in a situation that is best described as a 'Robinson Crusoe' experience – where the *Alien Visitor* became marooned on Earth in the same way as the hero of Daniel Defoe's novel *Robinson Crusoe* (1719) was shipwrecked and marooned on a desert island?

Perhaps the function of the pyramids was for protection purposes and for the *Alien Visitor* to record findings on Earth to be used by the *Alien Visitor* and its descendants to enable them to survive on Earth. Or maybe they were used to relay information to other *Alien Visitors* above the Earth. We know the pyramids were originally faced with brilliant white stones, which are believed to have been inscribed. But these have all since

---

[8] Screened 1998 and based on his book of the same name.
Quest for the Lost Civilisation - Heaven's Mirror Penguin Books 1999

disappeared. Maybe the bright stones with the inscriptions were a kind of encyclopaedia of all that the *Alien Visitor* had discovered on Earth. Or simply a 'message in a bottle' created by the stranded *Alien Visitor,* hoping to be discovered by one of its own kind.

It could be argued that all the work carried out and recorded on the smaller pyramids in Egypt and elsewhere around the planet was gathered together and used to build the Great Pyramid in the Giza complex in Egypt. As the largest pyramid, perhaps this was the one that could be seen and read by members of the *Alien Visitor* race back in outer space.

There are three reasons why I believe this Great Pyramid was particularly significant. The measurements that went into building it are very complicated which I deem to be the result of much research. It was built around one third of the way between the equator and the North Pole and at the centre of the world's habitable landmasses. This accuracy would require some detailed knowledge of Earth and hence astronomy and astrology. The variation between the sizes of each side of the base of the Great Pyramid is less than eight inches. It is unlikely that this choice of location could have come about by chance. The Great Pyramid is built on solid bedrock, which renders it virtually invulnerable to the severest earthquake and floods, as confirmed by its existence today. The height today is just a little over 137 m, the original pinnacle being missing. But mathematicians have calculated the original height of the pyramid using the existing base and the angles the base makes with what remains of the sides of the pyramid. These calculations have revealed that the true height of the Great Pyramid would have been 147.79 m. If the perimeter of the existing base is divided by the new height we get a figure that is twice that of *Pi*. *Pi* is a fundamental mathematical figure because it is the ratio of the circumference of a circle to its diameter and used in many calculations. This may be a coincidence, but perhaps it shows great intelligence in the construction of the Great Pyramid. *Pi* is applied to mathematical problems involving the lengths of arcs or other curves, the areas of ellipses, sectors, and other curved surfaces, and the volumes of solids. It is also used in various formulae elsewhere to describe such periodic phenomena as the motion of pendulums, the vibration of strings, and alternating electric currents. Perhaps the pyramid itself was used to solve mathematical problems. It does seem to show that its creators were competent at using mathematical equations which we have re-discovered and use today.

The second reason why I consider the Great Pyramid to be the most significant of all the pyramids is based on Peter Lemesurier's study[9]. He has found that some of the measurements of this pyramid match patterns on Earth. For example, he says the basic unit of measurement employed in the construction of the pyramid was a 'pyramid cubit' which is equivalent to 635.66 mm. The radius of the Earth from the centre to the pole is 6357 km. These measurements correspond on a scale of 10,000,000:1. The length of the pyramid side at the base is 365.242 pyramid cubits, a figure identical to the number of days in the solar tropical year. Furthermore, the mean distance of the Earth to the sun is about 149.5 million kilometres or 92,960,000 miles. The height of the Great Pyramid is 147.79 metres, which equals the

---

[9] Peter Lemesurier *The Great Pyramid Decoded* Element Books 1997

astronomical distance to the sun on a scale 1,000,000,000:1, with an error of only one per cent.

The final reason is the amazing subterranean chamber with a long shaft and deep well which was dug out of the solid rock before the pyramid was built on top. This suggests water was a critical component to this astonishing structure.

I am in no doubt the architects of Giza – and other structures that I believe were built at the same time – were well aware of constellations. Robert Bauval and Graham Hancock have explained in their book *Keeper of Genesis*[10], that if we were to turn the clock back to 10,500 BC – which we can do with the aid of computer technology – the complex at Giza can be seen to have mirrored the constellation Orion and the complex at Anqkor in Cambodia to have been designed in the image of the constellation Draco. I believe that the *Alien Visitor* may have used the insides of these pyramids to store information and findings that needed to be kept safe from the weather and other curious life-forms. Archaeologists have recently found shafts on the sides of the pyramids that could have been air vents. It seems odd that these structures, which are believed to have been built as burial chambers, would have air vents. I feel the vents indicate an earlier use by the *Alien Visitor*.

Various 'rhomboidal pits' have also been discovered at the Pyramids of Giza and near the Pyramid of Djedefra at Abu Roashste. Some were found to have boats in them. This indicates this area could have been a seaport with its boat building yards and dry-dock boat repair facilities. It is possible that a rapid change in

---

[10] Robert Bauval & Graham Hancock *Keeper of Genesis* Mandarin 1997

climate left this port high and dry and this area became dry and arid as it is today. The Sphinx could have been at the entrance to the harbour and visible from some distance, with the head much larger than it is today and possibly leonine to match the rest of its body.

But what would be the purpose of the accurately designed Pyramids at a seaport? Could this area at Giza have been an important junction comprising a sea and airport with the Sphinx a symbol for the conurbation that could be instantly recognised from the air and from the sea? The temples may have been arrival and departure lounges and the Pyramids craft hangers and air or space control towers. Or perhaps the pyramids were marker points for craft intending to land. This could have been a major administrative or commercial site for the *Alien Visitor*.

So, if the pyramids were part of the *Alien Visitor's* super port a main civilisation could be somewhere in close proximity. Perhaps it is buried beneath the sand following dramatic changes in climate and still to be discovered.

Another very impressive ancient complex at Tiahuanaco, near the southern shore of Lake Titicaca, in Bolivia was also built as a port. It has harbours, docks and quays, but today they cannot be used by any ship because Tiahuanaco is situated almost 4,000 m (13,000 ft) above sea level and is miles away from the nearest sea. I think the *Alien Visitor* established a network of colonies in different parts of the world and regular access to these colonies could be made using highly developed maritime skills. The discovery of maps dating back to 10,000 BC suggest the *Alien Visitor* was moving across, exploring and creating civilisations all over the world. The most impressive maritime civilisation in the ancient Mediterranean was that of Minoan Crete. Up until its demise around 1400 BC, following an invasion from mainland Greece, the Minoans were the masters of navigation in the Mediterranean and perhaps even in the entire world. Many historians believe that they owed their maritime expertise to an even greater maritime civilisation. And it could be argued that this Minoan culture, along with the civilisations in Egypt, Bolivia and possibly Wiltshire were either all created by the *Alien Visitor* or built on the site of or in the image of earlier *Alien Visitor* civilisations.

Unfortunately, little, if any proof of colonisation by an *Alien Visitor* with trade links across the globe seems to have survived. We cannot be certain what destroyed these civilisations or why the *Alien Visitor* left. Perhaps there was a disruption in the solar system, such as the explosion of a star or planet, which resulted in the bombardment of Earth by debris. This may have knocked Earth, dramatically altering it by causing all kinds of natural disasters such as earthquakes which split Earth's crust, violent super-volcanoes and prolonged storms and flooding. Any of these could have devastated the *Alien Visitor's* civilisations – or maybe just the headquarters – and forced them to leave the planet. Many cultures and religions across the world describe a devastating flood in early times. In fact, there are more than three hundred accounts of this flood, including the story about Noah in Genesis. Many academics believe this flood really happened.

In the BBC programme *The Great Flood*[11], Dr Bill Ryan and Dr Walter Pitman argue that around 7,500 years ago, the Bosporus – a narrow ribbon of water that joins the Black Sea to the Mediterranean – flooded the Black Sea. The pressure of rising sea levels caused by melting ice brought about this event. The swollen Black Sea devastated the civilisations which had grown up on what used to be its banks. But I conceive an event similar to this, also triggered by the melting ice from the Ice Age, took place much earlier in the Straits of Gibraltar or at the south end of the Red Sea. Recent geological evidence confirms that by 14,000 years ago, sea levels had surged by more than ten meters (30 ft). I am convinced that approximately two thousand years later, the increasing pressure of water on the Straits managed to break this natural dam, or this may have been caused by some sudden spectacular occurrence. Whatever the reason, water surged into the Mediterranean area increasing the levels of a number of smaller Mediterranean lakes eventually producing one large lake – the Mediterranean Sea. The creation of the Mediterranean Sea must have occurred before that of the Black Sea because the Mediterranean was closer to the already existing Atlantic Ocean which was rising. The extent of the flooding could have caused much of the *Alien Visitor's* civilisations to be submerged in much the same way as those settlements that had been swept away during the formation of the Black Sea. The water would have swept over the landmass including Egypt and Sudan before draining back into what is now the Mediterranean Sea and the Red Sea, leaving huge areas submerged in silt. After the flood, the only visible remains of the *Alien Visitor's* civilisations in this area were the pyramids and the head of the Sphinx.

---

[11] *The Great Flood* screened January 1999. Based on the book *Noah's Flood* by Dr Bill Ryan & Dr Walter Pitman Simon & Schuster 1999

As I have already said, its body bore the marks of erosion by water. It is also likely that the sands of Egypt still hold many secrets. We may have uncovered only a small amount of the pyramids and monuments in Egypt from this first civilisation. Whatever the reason for the devastation of the *Alien Visitor's* main civilisation in this area, it resulted in the breakdown of the network of civilisations, leaving any satellite colonies – which were not destroyed by the disaster – cut off from each other and isolated.

I am inclined to believe that the *Alien Visitor* was taken by surprise by this catastrophic flood or some other kind of natural disaster, or even with warning was unable to stop the devastation that occurred. The gigantic stone block left in the quarry near the ancient ruins of Baalbek in the northern end of the Syrian Dessert and the unfinished stonework discovered in other parts of the world indicates their sudden departure or demise.

Some of the children it produced with the *Homo sapiens* did survive in the satellite colonies and even in the damaged areas. Sumer, in what is now Iraq, is one of, what I believe to be, the earlier of this second wave of civilisations which sprung up following the departure of the *Alien Visitor*. It is thought to have been founded around 7,000 years ago. I think it may have been established by some of the survivors of the flood. Stone slabs, which are known as the Sumerian texts, have been found in the remains of this civilisation. Some of these tablets tell the tale of a survivor of a flood, which maybe suggests these people were aware of the flood. I believe that other tablets record some details of the earlier civilisations of the *Alien Visitor*. According to these Sumerian texts, a group of extra-terrestrial beings came into our solar system. Various texts portray them as very tall and often winged. The Sumerian tablets are dated around 4000 BC and accurately relate the stories of celestial planets that exist in our solar system complete with their moons, their dominant gaseous or aquatic features, their colours and their sizes, all of these being accurate. The tablets even record the existence of Pluto, Neptune and Uranus, planets which scientists believed were new discoveries made after 1700 AD. I think these tablets record the earlier arrival and teachings of the *Alien Visitor*. The people of Sumer write that God created them as a worker race. The tablets show that they believed they were there to serve Gods that came from the sky. This may have been our early ancestors' perception of the *Alien Visitor*. Did the *Alien Visitor* appear godlike with all its wisdom and space flight? If they were put to work by the *Alien Visitor* this may explain why they believed they had been created as a worker race.

We know from the tablets and artefacts recovered from Sumer that these people had great skills. They knew how to drain marshes for agriculture and develop trade. They set up industries based on the skills of weaving, leatherwork, metalwork, masonry, glass-making and pottery. Around 1900 BC, the Sumerians civilisation was in decline. Another race, the Amorites, conquered all of Mesopotamia. But the Sumerians left behind a number of tools and skills, including wheeled vehicles and potter's wheels, a system of writing, codes of law and city-states. They had also used large animals for work. Maybe they had developed all these skills when living with and working for the *Alien Visitor* before the flood and then used them to create their own civilisation.

The survivors would have settled in many areas apart from Sumer. Many of these early cultures share stories about a great flood. It could be argued that the survivors would have returned to Egypt and interpreted the remains of the first civilisation for their own purposes. Perhaps this first generation of survivors around the world were the direct children of the *Alien Visitor* and the *Homo sapiens* workers. This theory is supported by the discovery of graves in northern Egypt, which date back to a time preceding the rule of the pharaohs. The remains of people whose skulls were of greater size and whose bodies were larger than those of the natives were found in the graves. There are stories written around this time and later that tell of people who lived to great ages. The build and longevity of life of these early generations perhaps suggests they were different because they were the first to possess the *Alien Visitor* gene and perhaps they were more alien than *Homo sapiens*. At first the immediate descendants of the *Alien Visitor,* who survived the Flood, could have led the new civilisations and tried to maintain the culture of the *Alien Visitor*. But as this gene was spreading among a wider group of people, the earliest *Alien Visitor* children could have faced the threat of the growing intelligence of their own children. As the gene was dispersed to more and more generations, it seems the large gap in intelligence between the *Alien Visitor* and *Homo sapiens* workhorse closed and a new race made up of beings of similar intelligence was created.

Perhaps, as the generations continued to be born further away from the time of the occupation of the *Alien Visitor*, the stories of the *Alien Visitor* started to turn into legends and myths and the function of buildings such as the pyramids changed. Instead of making use of the air vents and storing information in the pyramids, most archaeologists believe the pyramids became used as a place for storing or laying the dead. The head of the Sphinx – which survived the flood – was re-carved. It is believed to have been fashioned in the image of Khafre, a king of Egypt. This reworking may explain why this part of the Sphinx does not carry marks caused by water erosion. The more these old constructions were used in a different way, the less it was remembered why they had been built in the first place. A modern analogy from the West is the desecration and sale of churches. Many have been converted into funeral parlours and some are even pubs! There is a chance that future generations may never be aware of the original purpose of these buildings. It seems as if these survivors and later generations of the second civilisation eventually only remembered that something significant had happened there but had no idea of what it could be. There are hundreds of references contained in old Egyptian texts, which tell us that the 'Gods' had concealed a great secret at the complex at Giza.

I believe we can see the remains of an *Alien Visitor* civilisation in Egypt. But is it possible that another part of the *Alien Visitor's* empire could still remain intact but is hidden under the Mediterranean Sea? There are many legends about the idea of a lost city. Celtic legends talk of a hidden and perfect city where everyone is free and never grows old. But the most famous stories about a hidden city are those which surround Atlantis. Plato is the first person who is believed to have written about Atlantis. He describes a city that flourished beyond the Straits of Gibraltar around 9000 BC, before sinking in "a single day of earthquakes, floods and rain." Scholars believe that Plato invented Atlantis as an allegory, which was aimed at warning his Athenian peers about the dangers of ambition. Despite this, Atlantis has been sought in many places including Sweden, Prussia, Palestine, Iran, Sri Lanka, Central Asia, Carthage, Crete, Santorini, Libya, Gibraltar, Bolivia, Mexico, Cornwall, Holland, France, Belgium, Spain, Portugal, Italy, Nigeria, Malta, Japan, Taiwan, the Caribbean Sea, the Caucasus Mountains, Russia's Azov Sea, India's Gulf of Khambhat and the mid-Atlantic. There are other settlements described on the tablets created by the Sumer people, which have never been found. Perhaps all these tales, which we have yet to prove, are not just myths, but describe a once-famous *Alien Visitor* settlement.

Maybe Atlantis had flourished over an enormous landmass incorporating many of the places mentioned above before it was destroyed and fragmented by the great Flood.

This dramatic flooding, which submerged much of the very beginning of civilisation, is explored by Graham Hancock in his book *Underworld*[12].

Maybe one day we will find parts of this metropolis in a good condition and untouched by other races since the Flood. This might give us proof of the *Alien Visitor's* time on our planet. Or perhaps there are already clues, which we have not yet learnt how to uncover, at the remains at Giza in Egypt or at Silbury Hill.

---

[12] Graham Hancock *Underworld* Michael Joseph 2002

Chapter 5

THE UNEXPLAINED PHENOMENA

I believe we can also find clues suggesting an *Alien Visitor* came to Earth if we examine unexplained phenomena.

In the UK, there are more than nine hundred stone circles. In England, a remarkable straight line has been traced from St Michael's Mount in Cornwall through Glastonbury and Avebury to Bury St Edmunds in Suffolk, while another runs from the north to south from the major Arbor Low stone circle in Derbyshire through Avebury and Stonehenge. Both these lines miss absolute straightness by a few hundred yards at a few points and we should not be surprised that over the centuries some land movement such as the mid-Atlantic rift could account for these particular discrepancies. It also appears that these lines extend through Scotland into the Orkney Islands and south into Brittany at a time when this was one landmass. These facts also suggest the sites may have been planned from above ground level and from the sky. Their positioning suggests knowledge of true east, west, north and south when they were built. Similarities in where these sites are built, comparable sizes and distances between stones at sites thousands of miles apart are too much of a coincidence to believe that this was not the work of a common influence. Similar kinds of building were going on around the world. In Peru, there is a collection of precise markings covering an area of 40 x 9 miles area, known as the Nazca lines. Thousands of these lines cross the desert between Nazca and Palpa. Some are more than five miles long, jumping deep ravines and cliffs, without altering their course. Others are zigzagged and spiral-shaped. Maria Reiche – who was an authority on the Nazca lines – found the 23 stone circles she studied in Britain were constructed using the same units of measurement. I think this gives us proof of architects using similar measurements and methods of construction thousands of miles apart. Perhaps this points to a universally- linked civilisation.

I have speculated as to why the various stone constructions were built around the world. They may have been points in an elaborate intergalactic compass, sextant or star map. They could have been used as links in an interstellar communications network. They may have been constructed to help the *Alien Visitor* fix its position in relation to the other planets in the galaxy or its own planet so that it would be able to chart a route when it wanted to leave Earth. One of the reasons the *Alien Visitor* might have built these structures could be that it arrived on Earth by mistake or following an accident and wanted to attract help to get home. It could be argued that these structures may have been a system of beacons, aimed at signalling to a passing ship, crewed by members of its own or a friendly planet. The beacons would have to be very large to be seen from space: a string of bonfires would be inadequate for this purpose. What would be required is some vast distinctive shape or pattern, which could be recognised by one of the *Alien Visitor's* rescuers circling our planet. The white horses which can also be found in the chalky hills in Wiltshire may also have been beacons or are modelled on original alien beacons. On the Nazca Plains of Peru there are other animal shapes – including a spider, monkey, whale, lizard and hummingbird – which I propose may have also been beacons, in the same way as Wiltshire's white horses. This suggests the *Alien Visitor* came from a planet with creatures similar to those on Earth. The *Alien Visitor's* familiarity with these creatures would have made it easier for the *Alien Visitor* to have known how to avoid dangers such as attacks or poisons. The *Alien Visitor* might have put up these beacons all over the world in order to make sure at least one was visible to the place the visitor came from so that there would never be a time when this appeal for help was obscured during the Earth's rotations. The *Alien Visitor* may have had to have recruited the *Homo sapiens* to build all these beacons.

We can put this idea to the test by taking a close look at one of the most famous stone circles – Stonehenge in Wiltshire. Stonehenge is different from all other known stone monuments because it was built in an area without stones! It was built at a time when our ancestors were hunters, struggling for survival and the only practical tools were made of stone, wood or bone. The big stones that form the distinctive circle, the ones that everyone notices when they look at Stonehenge are made of an incredibly hard sandstone called sarsen. It is the hardest rock in Britain, harder than granite, and is usually found lying around as big slabs. On Mohs scale, which measures resistance to abrasion, diamonds are 10, steel is 6 or 7 and sarsen stone is 7. It is not the sort of stone that is ever quarried. Bluestones were also used to build the circle. There are no known sources of bluestone anywhere in the vicinity. The closest source was in the

Preseli Mountains in West Wales, more than 225 km away. The puzzle is, how did the 82 bluestones get to Stonehenge? It is possible that a glacier could have picked up such a ragbag of stones, known as erratics and swept them to their final resting-place near the Stonehenge area. But this is unlikely as there no bluestones left in the area around Stonehenge.

Proof supporting the idea that the stones were transported by our ancestors to Stonehenge was provided in 1994 when one of the bluestones from Stonehenge was dated using a new method. When a rock is exposed to the atmosphere for the first time, either by erosion or by quarrying, it starts to accumulate an isotope of chlorine. Measuring the amount of this isotope gives the date when it was first exposed. In this instance the results showed that the bluestone rock from Stonehenge was only exposed about 14,000 years ago and this was, of course, years after the last Ice Age. If the bluestones were quarried at this time this could potentially make Stonehenge much older.

The question is why would a prehistoric tribe move giant boulders some 225 km outside the boundaries of their own territory? Perhaps the local tribe around Stonehenge got jealous at the impressive activity of other tribes' further north at Avebury or west at Stanton Drew and much like Chicago making sure it had bigger skyscrapers than New York, erected something technically more awesome than its neighbours. To build such grand complexes – which may have been much larger than what remains today, would have required a great deal of harmony, organisation, language and technology. These structures were fantastic, particularly as we know they were erected in a period where early humans lived in simple societies. Across the world, standing stones can be found. They come in various shapes, sizes and patterns. Some single megaliths have been found to be over 18 m (60 ft) high and weigh over 350 tons while others, much smaller, appear in their thousands in straight lines. I believe the local tribes were organised by a powerful outside influence, who understood the chemical properties of the stone and the reason for the construction and so ordered the tribes, so they travelled to the Preseli hills to bring back the stones. We cannot know for sure how these huge stones – some weighing more than 50 tons – were brought to Stonehenge. Perhaps they were built in position from a concrete type mixture poured into the wooden mould, or slid across a glacial landscape, or maybe conveyed and erected using levitation.

Levitation is a phenomenon that has interested us over the centuries. There have been examples of the rising of a human body off the ground, in apparent defiance of the law of gravity. The levitation of furniture and other objects during a séance has also been reported. Perhaps the *Alien Visitor* was able to draw upon gravitational forces or energies as yet untapped by modern science to levitate the rocks. Or maybe the *Alien Visitor* was able to move the stones using knowledge of phenomena, which we observe but do not yet understand, such as earth energy or ley lines. We understand ley lines are a source of energy similar to electricity when it hits the ground. We know the electricity must still be there but we have not yet worked out what it does or how it might be used by us. According to ancient Chinese science – which is based on a subtle conception of the order of nature far from our own today – there are currents or 'earth energy' within the Earth's surface. There have been cases where individuals have exhibited feats of exceptional strength way beyond the normal bounds – for example the mother being able to lift a car to recover her trapped child. This early science suggests earth energy can be magnified in the body and is called *chi*. Chinese traditional medicine has made a special study of this *chi* in the human body and the paths or meridians along which it runs and ways of correcting imbalances in the flow, by inserting needles at appropriate points on the meridian, to restore smooth running. Western medicine is only now coming to acknowledge that somehow it works. In the martial arts, the Chinese and Japanese, by working with this *chi* in the movements of the human body, can surpass mere physical force and weight. I believe the *Alien Visitor* may have known how to use these energy paths or how to channel their *chi* to their own advantage. Or perhaps the *Alien Visitor* knew how to use dowsing to achieve its own ends. Dowsing is not scientifically understood but some people can pick up very powerful reactions – using diving rods – particularly from the ground around these mysterious structures and even the stones themselves. Dowsers have detected straight lines meeting up at stone circles and even linking different megalithic sites, earthworks, pools, mounds and various landmarks, such as notches on the skyline. These lines have become known as ley lines. This energy is seen to flow not only through the planet, but also through all living organisms. The ley lines, then, are thought to form part of this network on the planetary scale. The megaliths are seen as not only marking this flow, but in some way storing, directing or channelling it, like a giant capacitor or diode to use electronics parlance.

Others see this energy as spiritual. Bell Rock, a towering red sandstone formation just south of Sedona, Arizona is an example of a vortex – a place where Earth's spiritual energies are concentrated and magnified and where psychic phenomena abound. People can feel vibrations, humming and swirling through their crystals and many report visions of their past lives as Native Americans, ancient Egyptians, Mayan princesses, major biblical figures and others. UFO activity is also associated with Bell Rock. Glastonbury Tor is considered to be Britain's premier vortex site and the town of Glastonbury is probably Sedona's nearest equivalent in Britain. These towns attract New Age travellers – a group which borrows most of its beliefs from Native American traditions, but also appropriates elements of Christianity, Hinduism, Buddhism, Zen, Taoism, astrology, the self-help movement and other esoteric beliefs.

If we accept, through the science of spectrometry, that all planets are composed of the same elements but in different quantities, then it might not be difficult to accept that all planets share some form of magnetic field. Perhaps the *Alien Visitor* was able to use the Earth's energy or ley lines because it was familiar with a similar phenomenon on its own planet. Perhaps, unlike us, the *Alien Visitor* had learnt to manipulate these sources of energy and used them to transport materials or to boost energy levels or used their own mode of transport to build beacons such as Silbury Hill.

It is likely that the *Alien Visitor* was well aware of these energies, but this knowledge became lost as the civilisation declined into evolutionary regression following its departure. But maybe we can observe evidence of it in action on Earth. The voyages of sea turtles thousands of miles along a Pacific 'highway' have been shown to be guided by a magnetic sense. Biologists have long suspected that the Earth's magnetic anomalies may be at the root of the leatherback turtles' spectacular navigational powers. Tracking them by satellite showed that they followed narrow corridors that are at most 100 miles wide – which is very narrow considering they have the whole Pacific Ocean in front of them. If the magnetic fields were scrambled then the turtles could not even begin their journey. On land, the migrating of Monarch butterflies has been discovered to use this magnetic sense to travel in their millions up to three thousand miles from the breeding grounds in Canada and California to spend winter in trees on mountainsides in central Mexico. The butterflies make the round trip once and despite being blown off course by winds they still make it to the same trees as their ancestors, by using these magnetic cues. And if the butterflies are screened from magnetic fields, like the turtles, they showed no consistent direction and therefore could not begin their amazing migration.

I believe that once the *Alien Visitor* had settled on Earth, the next priorities were those of communication and data recording. I think Silbury Hill was part of a significant complex in the *Alien Visitor's* attempts to communicate with the rest of its race. Our present-day communications and computer products rely on electricity generated using magnetic fields transmitted over power lines and cables. There does not appear to be any evidence of electrical power cables at this Wiltshire complex, but there is certainly plenty of evidence of forces and energy. Earth energy in the form of ley lines which can be traced using dowsing rods, criss-cross this area in abundance. It has been discovered that some of the stones at Avebury and Stonehenge in Wiltshire have magnetic properties. These stones are not from Wiltshire and the task of transporting them to the sites seems to have been arduous. Perhaps the people who built these stone structures needed them to hold magnetic properties which is why they did not use more accessible local stones. It is also a place where many crop circles are found which some believe are formed using the Earth's energy. Perhaps these circles are the *Alien Visitor's* messages being reflected back to Earth, similar to the way in which we beam signals off satellites that return to Earth.

So, from this ancient spacecraft-landing complex, could there still remain some residual energy from the transmission and reception of data some 13,000 years ago? Are we seeing in our crop fields some bits of information that cannot be 'received' properly because the 'hardware' is now in ruins? If this is so, what clues to our past and our future do these fragments of data hold?

Crop circles have been around for centuries. The first recorded crop circle was in Stirlingshire in 1678. It came to be known as the Devil's Circle. They have appeared by the hundreds each year all over the world. They are showing up fields of wheat, sugar cane, potatoes, sunflowers, oilseed rape, grass, in rice paddies. Similar phenomena also appear in pine forests, sand and mountain snow. Patterns appearing in mid-air which fragment before vanishing have also been reported. In the past, farmers and researchers were reluctant to draw attention to this phenomenon, so the subject was clouded in mystery, which added to the intrigue. However, from 1979 onwards in the vicinity of Silbury Hill, the circles have multiplied at a rate that can only be called explosive.

The increase in number of circles from around 100 a year in the eighties to more than 500 per year during the 1990s has attracted worldwide attention. Even the most sceptical of us are beginning to realise that something other than freaks of the weather, or hoaxers are responsible for this enigma. There are many theories to explain the existence of these patterns that seem to come from nowhere. Scientists around the world are studying various climatic effects, from weak weather fronts and atmospheric pressures causing summer whirlwinds, tornadoes, waterspouts and vortexes to luminous effects.

I saw the first 'Pictogram Circle' of 1990 that was formed at Cheesefoot Head in wheat on May 23. This configuration, which included four separate rectangular shapes, convinced me that phenomena such as vortexes could not produce these four identical rectangles. The appearance of these formations can be likened to those made by a mechanical typewriter where characters are stamped onto the page. This can be clearly seen in the many excellent aerial photographs and meticulous silhouette scale drawings of these circles in Lucy Pringle's book *Crop Circles: The Greatest Mystery of Modern Times*[13]. Although these patterns seem huge to us on Earth, they would be tiny – perhaps like small font letters – from the perspective of space from where they were sent.

Could the circles make up a form of language and how can these patterns be 'read'? Is each pattern a single character or a piece of a 'sentence'? Should we 'read' these patterns from top to bottom, left to right, inside or outside? It is important to keep photographic records of

---

[13] Lucy Pringle *Crop Circles The Greatest Mystery of Modern Times* Thorsons 1999

these circles in time and date sequence as, I hope that, one day knowledge of the meaning of these symbols will be revealed. I understand this is being done by an organisation known as CERES (Circles Effect Research) and the WCCSG (Wiltshire Crop Circle Study Group) and possibly the Ministry of Defence (MoD)?

If we can link this 'language' seen in the crop fields around Silbury Hill, with the symbols produced by the early prehistoric civilisation which sprang up around 13,000 years ago, then the evidence that these phenomena are linked with the creation of our first civilisations is irrefutable. Many are making comparisons between the crop circle patterns and symbols from old religions, alchemy, geometry, mathematics, hieroglyphics, astrology and ancient cultures. For example, on June 19, 1999 a near-perfect representation of a symbol associated with the Egyptians god Horus appeared in a wheat field near Silbury Hill. This could be a hoax but the Celts also incorporated symbols, found in crop fields, into their artwork on manuscripts, standing stones and artefacts. Examples include the Dunnichen Pictish stone. Designs like those of the Hopis of North America and Australian aborigines have appeared. Petroglyphs from Arctic Eskimo people and Tibetan Thangkas are reflected in the wheat.

One explanation for the explosion in the number of crop circles during the last decade can be attributed to hoaxers. Some have successfully demonstrated how to construct very complicated patterns, avoiding detection in the dead of night, with simple pieces of equipment, which leaves the rest of the crop in the field undisturbed. Many of the circles that started appearing in Wiltshire in 1979 can be attributed to local people. The activity of hoaxers, with their creative rural graffiti will continue to confuse the crop circle enigma. But it remains bewildering how many of the more intricate designs can be created so perfectly and so quickly in the dead of night or in the middle of the day. What we need is a well-documented scientific study of circles which we believe have not been made by humans. This obviously, would be very difficult to compile but there are many circles that are unexplained and we do not know for certain how they got into fields. Groups studying the crop circles have found differences between a formation known to have been produced by hoaxers and other formations whose origin is unclear. A true design is said to reveal bent and twisted but not broken intricately woven stems and correct geometry. Inside the circle, it has been claimed strong energetic currents can be felt, which occasionally cause equipment – such as cameras, video recorders and mobile phones – to fail. Others have found small and equally puzzling 'grapeshot' circles in close proximity to a 'real' formation. From the many aerial photographs taken there seems to be little or no distortion to the shape of the formation in spite of steep slopes and undulations in some of the fields where they appear.

In the book *The Corn Circle Enigma*[14] which is written by the group which formed the Centre for Crop Circle Studies, (the CCCS) there is a very interesting photograph which shows a mixture of round outlines of prehistoric burial mounds now flattened, which had become visible in the very dry spring in 1988, with a number of crop circles, suggesting a link between these ancient sites and the crop circles. Ever since seeing my

---

[14] Ralph Noyes *The Crop Circle Enigma* Gateway Books 1991

first crop of circles opposite Silbury Hill in July 1988, I have been intrigued by their appearance from 'out of nowhere'. My first crop circle was a 'quintuplet'. Eleven days later a second 'quintuplet' had mysteriously appeared in the same field. Many who witness a circle are immediately drawn to the mystical, the paranormal and the extra-terrestrial and set out to try to solve the puzzle – and I am one of many.

I believe, the appearance of the 'Chilbolton Code' and the 'Chilbolton Face', in a wheat field on the grounds of the Chilbolton radio telescope facility near Wherwell in Hampshire in August 2001, and the 'Scary Alien', more than 100 metres long, which appeared in a wheat field at Crabwood near Winchester, Hampshire in August 2002, represent a substantial step forward and puts an end to earlier speculation that climatic anomalies or hoaxers are responsible for every crop formation. In my view, it seems unlikely that the appearance of these complex formations, which show faces and hieroglyphics, could be caused by tornadoes, or man-made with a ball of string and plank of wood. So what can be the explanation for these crop formations?

I think that when the *Alien Visitor* was on this planet, some 13,000 years ago, it was developing a way of transmitting and receiving messages inside and outside Earth. I believe that even though the *Alien Visitor* eventually left our planet, these signals or channels of communication may still be 'live'. The crop circles may be the result of messages being sent on this 'live channel'. Of course, because we do not know what the messages mean it is, so far, impossible to know whether the *Alien Visitor* is still trying to communicate with us or is unwittingly using a 'live' channel. Perhaps the reason these crop circles appear near locations such as Silbury Hill and Avebury is because these sites were constructed to make transmission and reception possible. If something catastrophic were to happen to us, we would also leave behind millions of signals of varying frequencies and wavelengths that would remain in the ether indefinitely or until a method of receiving these signals had been reproduced accidentally or by design.

Although crop circles have been around for hundreds if not thousands of years, it seems that in more recent times the number and complexity of these formations have increased dramatically. For whatever reasons it seems the 'live channel' is being used more frequently and with more skill. Perhaps the answers to our questions about alien life on Earth are about to be resolved.

As well as further new archaeological discoveries of ancient cities, Atlantis perhaps, or recovery of hidden artefacts locked away in museums, monasteries or the Vatican; or archaeologists and geneticists working together on investigating the DNA in ancient mummified remains; or the slow recovery of our hidden knowledge we have inherited from the offspring of the *Alien Visitor* and the bipedal *Hominid* species; or the arrival of a UFO with the return of the *Alien Visitor;* these 'messages' which were transmitted by the *Alien Visitor* when it lived on our planet that are appearing in crop fields, could also offer us clues to the existence of the *Alien Visitor* on Earth.

I think we already have some opportunities for deciphering the 'messages' appearing in the crop fields because we have the *Alien Visitor* gene and therefore a memory from the *Alien Visitor*. It is possible that we could be unknowingly accessing this subconscious memory when we transmit messages so it follows that, by looking at the way we send and receive messages we might be able to understand how the *Alien Visitor* did the same.

For example, in 1974 a message was beamed from a radio telescope in Arecibo, Puerto Rico, aimed at a star cluster called M13. This cluster is about 23,000 light years from Earth and any reply can only be expected 40,000 years from now, at the earliest. However, the appearance of the 'Chilbolton Code' has attracted media coverage because it bears a resemblance to the image sent from Puerto Rico. Some newspapers have speculated that this crop formation is proof that our message has already been received. But this seems impossible because our message should only be at the start of its very long journey to M13; unless an alien spacecraft had intercepted this message not long after it had started its journey?

But I sense the real significance of the similarity between the M13 message and 'Chilbolton Code' is that we seem to be subconsciously creating the kind of images which are being transmitted to Earth on the 'live channel'.

If we continue to study these crop formations, we may start to understand the information the *Alien Visitor* communicates. This research may finally provide us with the answer to why the *Alien Visitor* came to Earth and what it achieved while on this planet. By comparing the subtle differences between the message we sent to M13 and the 'Chilbolton Code', perhaps we can unlock the meaning of similar extra-terrestrial transmissions that are being beamed onto Earth.

By analysing the crop formations in the context of how we send and receive messages maybe we can understand how to decipher them.

One place where we could start is by looking at how and why we use binary codes so much in our communications.

A computer translates the striking of the '**?**' symbol on the keyboard as an 8-bit binary code 00111111 that represents the digital signal for '**?**', which conforms to the ASCII (American Standard Code for Information Interchange) convention. This string of '0's and '1's is easily handled by the computer as '0' = no pulse and '1' = a pulse of electricity. Prior to the '**?**' being displayed on the computer screen the translation process is reversed and the '**?**' symbol is then displayed on the screen or sent to an email recipient and **NOT** the digital signal 00111111. Similar principles apply to radio and television broadcasts, where radio and television sets are the receivers, which are also rapidly changing from analogue to digital technology.

But is there another subtler means of transmitting and receiving extra-terrestrial 'messages'? Can the explanation quite simply be that these 'messages are being channelled through some of us? We readily accept the artists' talent to 'receive' portraits or landscapes in their conscious memory or images from their unconscious or subconscious memory and 'transmit' these pictures to paper or canvas.

Some crop formation researchers believe that the meanings of crop formations can be channelled through the minds of some of our fellow human beings. Some 'channellers', also known as mediums, attribute a universal 'star' symbol along with a meaning for each formation. Is this the beginning of a universal language lesson from the extra-terrestrials?

Are hoaxers the unwitting transceivers for these extra-terrestrial 'messages' contained in their subconscious memories, which they reproduce as crop formations? Many hoaxers who have planned and created crop formations have confessed to becoming more and more convinced that paranormal forces are working through them.

Later in the book, I investigate the idea that within our own physical makeup we have a gene from the *Alien Visitor* and a capacity for a greater understanding of everything that constituted this *Alien Visitor*. I look at how, as a race, we only have glimpses of the possibilities offered by this gene. It is possible to argue that perhaps all crop circles are extra-terrestrial and that even those which hoaxers admit to making have been made out of a compulsion in the hoaxer to use the knowledge contained in their inherited alien gene.

Is the true significance of crop circles that they provoke a mind enhancing experience by getting us as individuals to throw back into ourselves? Is this a subtle way of getting each and every one of us to explore our subconscious memory and discover just how remarkable we all are.

Is it a coincidence that crop formations are appearing in clusters around the ancient monuments which are still visible, e.g. Avebury (incorporating Silbury Hill), Stonehenge, and those monuments that have long since disappeared?

Did the extra-terrestrial(s) have the opportunity to perfect a means of transmitting information using its higher intelligence and Earth's resources, before they and their 'equipment' were destroyed or damaged in the natural disaster that resulted in the great flood? I can only assume from the complexity of the ancient civilisations that it had. So, should we expect to see more elaborate patterns, pictures and even messages, by whatever means, which may provide the answer to this mystery that confounds us? I think we will - so sit back and enjoy the next instalment!

My theory accepts unequivocally the existence of other life on other planets, some of which arrived on Earth around 13,000 years ago. As the stone circles and mounds remain on Earth and crop formations continue to be created perhaps, we are unwittingly continuing to transmit to and receive messages from the *Alien Visitor's* race every day. Maybe we are, unknowingly, organising another meeting in the future. Perhaps an increase in crop formation activity is an indication that the *Alien Visitor* is preparing to return to Earth.

Chapter 6

PYRAMIDS

Pyramids are the most ancient and mysterious monuments found on Earth and may provide some important clues to the *Alien Visitor* Gene Theory.

In Wiltshire, near the stone circles at Avebury, stands Silbury Hill. This ancient enigmatic mound has provided the background for a number of UFO sightings and many of the less obvious man-made crop circles in recent years.

Are there any clues to show that Silbury Hill is linked to extra-terrestrials and our human evolution? I believe a conceivable explanation for the purpose of Silbury Hill can be found by studying the most ancient and mysterious monuments found on Earth – pyramids!

The perception we have of Silbury Hill is that of a 4,500 year old ceremonial mound, inspired by 'ritual' and built by our Pagan/Druid pre-Christian ancestors. This is mainly thanks to archaeologist Professor Richard Atkinson and the BBC following the dig from 1968-1970, and subsequently endorsed by English Heritage.

There were no records made of this exploration. However, the dig, sponsored by the BBC to produce a series of gimmicky archaeology programmes, heavily promoted an item which was found near the surface early on in the dig – an antler. The antler was subsequently radiocarbon dated to around 4,500 years and became a headline or 'breaking news' item. To embellish the story it was decided that the antler was used as a pick in the construction and the huge illogical leap was made - Silbury Hill must also be approximately 4,500 years old!!

Most people are surprised to learn that there is, in fact, no way to directly determine the age of any fossil or rock. The so called 'absolute' methods of dating (radiometric methods) actually only measure the present ratios of radioactive isotopes and their decay products in suitable specimens - not their age. These measured ratios are then extrapolated to an 'age' determination. Despite its obvious appeal to archaeologists, most radiocarbon facilities date bone only rarely. The principal reason is often poor preservation of collagen in many contexts. Preservation of bone collagen is influenced principally by the environment within which the bone is deposited, and, specifically, by the interrelated influences of pH, microbial activity, temperature, and water. However, these digenetic influences can be extremely variable between, and within, sites. In general, there is a broad gradient in the preservation state of bones from those deposited in warmer, more humid environs to those recovered from archaeological contexts in colder, more temperate climes. Over many years, it has become apparent that the characterisation of the quality of the extracted 'collagen' is crucial to validate the accuracy of the obtained 14C determinations. Several methods of achieving this have been tried but few 14C laboratories regularly apply the range of analytical measurements necessary to provide minimum assurance for submitters of bone samples (e.g. C to N ratios) even when the samples are of crucial importance to studies of late human evolution.

The bottom line is that radiometric dating procedures don't provide the consistent absolute dating method we would like to have. It therefore seems unlikely that modern radiocarbon dating techniques can so accurately date the Silbury Hill antler to 4,500 years - and this is accepting the huge assumption it was used as a pick in its construction!

But Atkinson also left another legacy, an unstable English Heritage monument, and collapses at the top of the hill spurred English Heritage to embark on a Conservation and Restoration Project in 2007/2008.

Although much of the evidence of its age and function had been contaminated over the centuries, there was some evidence discovered during this recent dig to suggest that Silbury Hill was originally constructed as a pyramid.

Some of the uncovered information to suggest this extraordinary pyramid possibility is as follows:-

- Close to the entrance a large chamber had been discovered and its purpose unknown. (*Figure 1*) Other cavities have been discovered beneath the base of the Hill. Does this suggest evidence of a storage place but any artefacts placed within had long since been removed and any records lost?

- A thin band of dark brown butter-textured material approximately 5mm thick appears to have covered the base area prior to the construction. So far no stones have been found in this bizarre sheet of mica-like material. (*Figure 2*) It is likely that the sheet was cut as a square to the size of the base and carefully aligned to the four cardinal directions. The material may have the properties of sheet mica (Illite, Muscovite or Glauconite) which is used as a dielectric in capacitors which in electronics are used to hold electric charge. Mica can also be used as an insulator.

- Large chalk blocks measuring 29 x 39½ x 12 pyramid inches were discovered at the top of Silbury Hill. (*Figures 3 & 4*)

  "Over 10,000 survey points on the mound alone allowed us to plot detailed contours. This emphasised that the structure is not in fact circular, but built in straight segments that may indicate radial walls or buttresses"

  English Heritage

- There were large sarsen stones found at the summit and a number of pieces have been discovered at the base and close to the surface elsewhere in the Hill. (*Figure 5*) These large sarsen stones suggest a cap or podium at the top of the structure.

- A few flint flakes some dated to 12,000 years old were discovered in pits on top of the first phase at the centre of Silbury Hill. (*Figure 6*) The alternative theory expounded by many independent researchers including myself that suggests Silbury Hill is much older, may also prove impossible to confirm. As much as I would like to use flint flakes dated to 12,000 years old, found in pits at the top of the first phase in the construction of Silbury Hill as a possible date stamp, but for the reasons already mentioned, there is also some incongruity when arriving at this conclusion. Also the flint flakes may have been scooped up unintentionally from the landscape and deposited unknowingly in the centre during its construction?

- The building of the final phase of the Hill occurred in "steps".

Archaeologists found this to be a very 'clean' site, suggesting that once Silbury Hill had been built, it seems unusual that only a selected few had access to the Hill.

[15]Jim Leary, English Heritage chief archaeologist on this restoration project, gives an account of his research and reiterates the traditional views for the age, construction and purpose of Silbury Hill in his beautifully presented and well documented book *The Story of Silbury Hill*.

To their immense credit much more information was collected and recorded by English Heritage archaeologists for future scientists to study. It is clear that in our distant past there was a mass of people in this area who were organised and prepared to work very hard in relative harmony, but we can still only guess at its function.

What happened to this autocratic regime, those architects able to organise and bring together large numbers of people to build a huge complex encompassing monuments such as the Avebury Stone Circle, Stonehenge and Silbury Hill which archaeologists suggest were built around the same time?

Prior to and since standing at the centre of Silbury Hill in October 2007, (*Figure 7*) I have been involved with scientists and researchers around the world studying

---

[15] Jim Leary, Archaeologist   *The Story of Silbury Hill*   English Heritage 2010

mounds similar to Silbury Hill - from the newest in Bosnia and China to the most famous in Egypt.

We are aware of the Great Pyramid in Egypt but what is not fully understood is the existent of hundreds if not thousands of pyramids built on every continent on Earth.

During World War II a US Air Force pilot James Gaussman was flying between China and India, his report to an intelligence officer is very interesting:

"I banked to avoid a mountain and we came out over a level valley. Directly below was a gigantic white pyramid. It looked like something out of a fairy tale. It was encased in shimmering white. This could have been metal, or some sort of stone. It was pure white on all sides. The remarkable thing was the capstone, a huge piece of jewel-like material that could have been crystal. There was no way we could have landed, although we wanted to. We were struck by the immensity of the thing."

With the recent rapid development of the computer and communications technologies (World Wide Web, satellite, etc), many pyramids hitherto unknown are now being carefully studied.

So far over 300 mounds have been found in China. Many mounds of similar shape and size to Silbury Hill were excavated to expose a stepped pyramid or podium beneath the soil and vegetation. Some had chambers buried inside and/or beneath the construction. Water close by was familiar to all sites.

In Europe, pyramids have recently been unearthed in the Canary Islands, Sardinia, Sicily, France, Greece and Italy.

Many 'unusual' hills where monumental structures are believed to be hiding under the soil haven't been excavated because of the cost. An example is Piramida Hill (50m) in Maribor, Slovenia which has been known by this name from time immemorial and no one knows why!

There are not only small ancient pyramids, but also monumental, colossal structures hidden under hills, for example the Pyramid of the Sun, discovered in 2005 near Visoko in Bosnia & Herzegovina.

So, what was so important about the pyramid structure and its properties that so many were built in our prehistory!?

To discover more, we must first understand the scientific and technological properties of the pyramid. A short experiment with a suspended cardboard pyramid from a piece of thread gives some clues to the properties of the pyramid. What happens when I clasp my hands and point my fingers at the motionless pyramid? Although these experiments don't meet the rigors of scientific experimentation, energy appears to be spiralling through the pyramid causing it to rotate – sometimes clockwise sometimes anticlockwise. Why does the suspended pyramid rotate?

Clues to this mystery can be found thanks to the discovery of the atom and its constituent parts which enabled the development of electricity by 19th century inventors including Westinghouse, Edison and Tesla. The motion of negatively charged electrons in one direction and positively charged in the other around an electric circuit known as an electric current is clearly understood. What is less familiar is the flow of ionic energy around our planet. Ions occur when an atom either gains an electron (anion) or looses an electron (cation). Ions exist naturally due to the ongoing atomic reactions with energy sources such as heat, light and sound energy. An ionic current flows when the negatively charged anions are attracted towards the positively charged (opposites attract) Sun via the ionosphere and the positively charged cations are attracted from the Sun to the negatively charged Earth. This flow of ionic current is a natural occurring wireless phenomenon.

However, if a pyramid shape is placed on the ground thus intersecting this flow of ionic current, its effect is to dramatically increase the flow of electrical energy at the tip of the pyramid compared to the base, i.e. the pyramid is able to generate and store free electrical energy! The simple experiment clearly shows that energy has been produced as revealed by the rotation of the suspended pyramid!

All pyramids have been found to contain some crystalline/quartz stone such as sarsen, granite or salt. These materials act as a transducer. A transducer is a power transforming device which can convert one form of energy into another, (e.g. microphone, turbine, windmill, etc). A pyramid depending on its size, angle, construction and materials used (Professor Atkinson described Silbury Hill as being inside 'an enormously complicated and highly coloured layer cake') - can generate huge amounts of electrical energy which can be converted into large magnetic fields, Ion Generator/Bionizer (as found in modern air purifiers/conditioners), heat and earth (ley line) energy. The piezo-electric transducer based upon the properties possessed by certain crystalline/quartz materials previously mentioned can also convert the electrical energy into acoustic energy, and vice versa. They have been used as the basic element of oscillators to provide very-high-frequency stability above about 20 kHz) in transmitters (seismic communication signals) and in electronic measuring equipment.

The first practical application for piezoelectric devices was sonar, first developed during World War I. In France in 1917, Paul Langevin and his coworkers developed an ultrasonic submarine detector. The detector consisted of a transducer, made of thin quartz crystals carefully glued between two steel plates, and a hydrophone to detect the returned echo. By emitting a high-frequency chirp from the transducer, and measuring the amount of time it takes to hear an echo from the sound waves bouncing off an object, one can calculate the distance to that object.

The Pyramid shape (*Diagram 2*) has been proved to convert earth/ley line energy into seismic (acoustic) waves in a wide range of frequencies as shown in the record of fluctuations of seismic emission envelope in the center of the Red Pyramid at Dashur. Scientists have measured seism acoustic waves (*Diagram 1*) which emanate from the tip of the pyramid and have discovered that all pyramids, including the famous pyramids at Giza, produce their own seism acoustic emission or unique transmission signal! They also discovered that seism acoustic emission is accompanied by electromagnetic radiation.

In the field of Ion Generator/Bionizers, we now have Speleotherapy clinics - the benefits were first described in a book published by a Polish physician in

1834 who took patients with respiratory diseases and breathing difficulties down into salt mines for cures.

It became a standard feature of spa treatments in Eastern Europe. People suffering from respiratory diseases have been visiting salt caves for relief since the Middle Ages, and this traditional natural remedy is widely used in Russia and the Ukraine. All modern air conditioning systems have negative ion generators.

Water nearby, which is common to all pyramids, provides a constant source of negative anions. Comparing a torch with a pyramid, the pyramid uses the infinite negative charge from earth which acts as a huge battery compared to the small alkaline battery in the torch!

A summary of other interesting features common to all pyramids discovered on every continent on Earth are as follows:-

Δ The positioning of the pyramid is purposely selected with a special regard for mathematics and the cosmos.

Δ The corners of the pyramid accurately point to the four cardinal directions of North, South, East and West or reflect the two equinoxes and the two solstices.

Δ Pyramids are carefully planned and constructed in a step formation. Even the carefully positioned blocks are deliberately turned with the flat side out.

Δ Ley line/earth energies bisect the pyramid.

Δ They all contain crystalline stones. Crystal is a transducer of electrical and mechanical energy. A transducer is a power transforming device which converts one form of energy into another.

∆ The pyramid shape containing crystalline stone, acts as a giant crystal piezoelectric transducer. This converts earth/ley line energy, in the form of negative ions from underground water, into seismic (acoustic) waves in a wide range of frequencies. Each pyramid has its own unique emitting frequency.

∆ Cavities, passages, chambers and anti-chambers are found inside and beneath the base of the pyramid.

∆ Each pyramid contains 'inherited' items which over the centuries have been open to many misinterpretations.

The material used in the original construction of the pyramid, the climatic conditions endured over the centuries and the respect (or otherwise) shown by the peoples living with these monuments, determines the condition, size, shape and even if the pyramid still exists.

Was there an extra-terrestrial race who understood the properties of pyramids and the science of our planet?

Were pyramids built because they were critical to their survival and the continued existence of their offspring – us!! Their amazing mathematical and astrological knowledge suggest they did?

Is this another crackpot idea? Russian scientists don't think so. They are building pyramids to purify the surrounding atmosphere to help tackle the effects of greenhouse gasses. Maybe one day we will see pyramid power used to replace wind farms!?

Was Silbury Hill originally built as a pyramid? The evidence from my research suggest Silbury Hill was indeed built as a pyramid and part of a huge complex incorporating Avebury Stone Circles nearby, the recently excavated Marden Henge to the west and Stonehenge to the south.

Did pyramids play a vital part in our early evolution? Plans are being discussed by Scientists for a "Doomsday Ark" on the Moon that will contain the essentials of life and civilization, to be activated in the event of Earth being devastated by a giant asteroid or nuclear war.

A basic version of the "ark" would contain hard disks holding information such as DNA sequences and instructions for metal smelting and planting crops. The plan to place these items in a vault just under the lunar surface and transmitters above the vault would send the data to heavily protected receivers on Earth. If no receivers survived, the "ark" would continue transmitting the information until new ones could be built.

In my *Alien Visitor* gene theory I suggest our knowledge has been inherited from an alien ancestor. We have acquired the *Alien* memory of its life on Earth together with its own history going back to when the *Alien* life first evolved on some distant planet!

Everything we imagine or have yet to imagine has already happened in our *Alien* history. In other words, we are mimicking the evolution of the *Alien Visitor*. The *Alien Visitor's* history is our future. There will be anomalies because we are evolving on Earth and the *Alien Visitor* evolved on a different planet so this may force us to evolve in a slightly different way from the *Alien Visitor*.

So, if we are slowly recovering this alien knowledge, can we find clues to early human evolution in our modern ideas and inventions? Are we repeating the idea of a "Doomsday Ark" from knowledge contained in our inherited memory? Will pyramids play a key role in our future advancement with the likelihood that it will be the first structure to be built on the Moon?

Does Silbury Hill display the hallmarks of a previous "Doomsday Ark" built on Earth by extra-terrestrial surveyors around 12,000 years ago? If Silbury Hill was originally built as a pyramid this would provide a remarkable link to other pyramids and to our highly intelligent ancestors that existed in our prehistory?

Are we becoming more consciously aware of the existence of our extra-terrestrial heritage? If our extra-terrestrial ancestors return will we have some common knowledge that will enable us to understand the secrets of space and our hidden powers?

Silbury Hill

In Wiltshire, near the stone circles at Avebury, stands *Silbury Hill*. This ancient enigmatic mound has provided the background for a number of UFO sightings and many of the less obvious man-made crop circles in recent years.

Silbury Hill, surrounded by water, located close to the A4 near Avebury, Wiltshire, UK

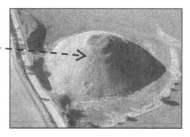

Aerial view of Silbury Hill   ©Babz Bell

Silbury Hill in the distance with a crop circle nearby.

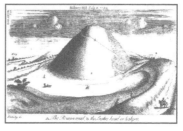

Silbury Hill as depicted in a sketch by William Stukeley in 1723

Silbury Hill – A White Pyramid?

Findings from the English Heritage Conservation and Restoration Project 2007-2008 suggest Silbury Hill maybe more than a chalk mound, a spoil heap from the ditches dug at the nearby standing stones at Avebury.

English Heritage and civil engineering partner Skanska at the Silbury Hill Project Site in 2008

Figure 1 Mysterious chamber beneath the base of the Hill, facing in an N ↔ S direction

Figure 2 Jim Leary, English Heritage archaeologist, examining the mysterious layer of dark brown butter-textured material discovered between the foundation and the chalk

Figure 3 Intriguingly, in spite of being weathered and damaged over time to look like a dry stone wall, these stones/bricks from the top of Silbury Hill could be measured, i.e. 74cm high x 1m wide x 30cm thick (29 x 39½ x 12 pyramid inches).

Figure 4 A scale model of a chalk block/brick found at the summit

Figure 5 Many pieces of sarsen stone have been found close to the surface of the mound. Was this part of a cap at the apex of the white stepped Silbury Pyramid?

Figure 6 Flint flakes 12,000 years old found in small pits on the top of the first phase of the construction

The final pyramid construction, standing on top of a chalk spur, at least 40m high and clearly visible particularly from the sky……..

…… or maybe the large pieces of sarsen stone confirm an obelisk on top of a stepped white podium similar to the Nyuserre solar temple at Abu Gurab, Egypt?

Figure 7 Author at the centre of Silbury Hill on Wednesday 24th October 2007

Pyramid Mounds

Pyramids and their remains in mounds have been discovered on every continent on Earth.

A denuded 'Silbury Hill' found next to the Bent Pyramid in Dashur, approximately 40 kilometres south of Cairo.

Pyramid examples from Egypt of what Silbury Hill may have looked like beneath the lush vegetation.

Silbury Hill has often been compared with King Djoser's step pyramid at Saqqara

Silbury Hill – Pyramid Mound? Artistic impression in watercolour by the Author.

Bosnian Pyramid of the Sun – is this the largest natural pyramid on Earth?

Pyramid Technology

What was so important about the pyramid structure and its properties that hundreds, if not thousands, were built on every continent on Earth in our prehistory!?

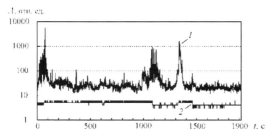

© Dr Oleg Khavroshkin, Head of Nonlinear Seismology Lab, Russian Academy of Sciences, Schmidt Institute of Physics of the Earth

Diagram 2 Pyramid shape has been proved to convert earth/ley line energy into seismic (acoustic) waves in a wide range of frequencies as shown in the record of fluctuations of seismic emission envelope in the center of the Red Pyramid at Dashur

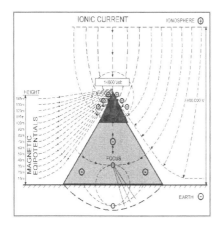

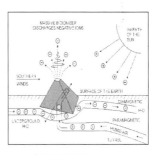

© Hrvoje Zujić

Production of 'energy of the universe', key to human development and to the rapid growth of plants and crops in the near vicinity

Diagram 1 If a pyramid shape is placed on the ground thus intersecting this flow of ionic current, its effect is to dramatically increase the flow of electrical energy at the tip of the pyramid compared to the base, i.e. the pyramid is able to generate and store free electrical energy!
Transducers discovered in all pyramids can convert the huge amounts of electrical energy into other forms of energy including magnetic and Ion Generator/Bionizer, i.e., air purifiers/conditioners.
The diagram shows a sarsen stone transducer cap to the pyramid, with a Mica sheet covering the base acting as a possible insulator?

Chapter 7

PROBING THE MIND

As far back as we can penetrate into the beginning of man's thinking, we find that he recognised a difference between mind and matter and he placed mind in a more exalted realm than matter. As man developed, the idea of mind as an exclusive human possession and distinct from matter became clearer.[16]

I believe the *Alien Visitor* made us into the race we are today by boosting our intelligence beyond that of other creatures on Earth. We have developed from cavemen to cosmonauts. Perhaps, if we study our intelligence, we may find some clues about our extra-terrestrial ancestor.

I also believe our intelligence is closely associated with the information stored in our memory and the ease with which we can access this information. In other words, intelligence is a measure of the ease in which we can access, use and develop this 'hidden' knowledge stored in our conscious, unconscious and subconscious memory. In a computer analogy, it is as though a very high capacity and fully utilised hard disk has been compressed to the size of a cell or gene which has been passed down to us through our genetic inheritance. Each generation discovers new or additional information in a similar way to accessing data on the hard disk in a computer system. Accessing the innermost secrets of our

---

[16] S. E. Frost Jr. *Basic Teachings of the Great Philosophers* Bantam Doubleday 1962

memory is key and many methods have been tried over the centuries, from fasting to drug taking. Computer 'hackers' have demonstrated how secret' data can be retrieved, but so far we have yet to discover how to 'hack' into our hidden memory banks.

If it were possible to produce a genealogical chart from the birth of the first *Alien Visitor* and *Homo sapiens* hybrid, it would produce offspring with varying levels of the *Alien Visitor* gene as each generation was born.

The 1990s were designated the Decade of the Brain. The idea was to promote research into the brain and disseminate all the information we are gleaning about our most secretive body part, to the widest audience possible. Hardly a day goes by without the announcement of a discovery associated with the brain.

A living brain inside the skull looks pretty much like any other brain in terms of general shape and configuration of the constituent regions. The male brain weighs an average of 1,347g compared to the female brain at 1,223g. Men excel in cognitive tests which include visuo-spatial tasks such as mental rotation of figures, map-reading, remembering positions of numbers. At one point in our evolution the abilities revealed by such tests and hence the larger brain could have been important in finding females. Modern research begins to question this as women's navigational skills are shown to be equal to their male counterparts. The upper part of our brain is comprised of two identical looking halves or hemispheres. In most people, the left half is associated with language, logic, lists, number, linearity, and analysis. The right half deals with rhythm, imagination, colour, daydreaming, spatial awareness, Gestalt (whole picture) dimension and fun. Studies have shown that the more we use both sides of our brain, then the more effective our overall brain performance is. Many of the great minds of our times used both sides of their brains. The cortex – the site of human perception and intelligence, is a layer of grey matter that constitutes the outer layer of the cerebrum. It is several centimetres thick and has a surface area of about 2,000 square cm (310 square inches), owing largely to an elaborate series of convolutions in the brain surface. Similarly, the basic building block, the neuron (brain cell), is common to all. However, it is in the middle layer, in the micro circuitry of neurons, that our individual experiences and predisposition's can be most sensitively reflected. Although we are born with all the neurons we are ever going to have - in each human brain there are an estimated one million, million (1, 000, 000, 000, 000) neurons - it is the connections between those cells that proliferate to an astonishing degree in the first few years of life and which can be modified by experience. Hence even identical twins will not have identical brains. An individual is not an inflexible mental monolith, but is forever evolving, never experiencing the same moment of consciousness twice.

Understanding the properties and purpose of a neuron and how it relates to other neurons is crucial to understanding the brain. Neurons are biological signalling mechanisms. They pass messages back and forth through the brain and the nervous system by means of chemicals that influence neighbouring and sometimes far-distant cells. The points of connection between neurons are at infinitesimally small gaps, called synapses, where the exchange of chemical signals takes place. A single neuron can possess as many as 20,000 synapses on its dendrites – threadlike extensions of a nerve cell. Every neuron is different from every other neuron in its shape, as trees and plants vary in the forest. As Gerald Edelman, the Nobel prize-winning brain scientist puts it:

The workings of the brain more closely resemble the living ecology of a jungle than they do the activities of a computer or any machine we could possibly imagine.

Yet the brain is like no other jungle known on Earth. It is as if neurons spread out their tentacles not only to attach themselves to neighbours, but also to communicate with plants 1,000 miles distant. Just as stunning are the numerical properties of these nerve cells. Take the cerebral cortex, responsible for language, thought, complex movement patterns and activities such as appreciation of music. If one were to flatten out the cortex, it would end up the size of a small tea towel and just as thick. Contained within its structure are an estimated ten billion neurons. Yet, amazingly, the neurons' branches create a hyper astronomical number – of the order of ten followed by millions of zeros – with the variously combined connections with other neurons. Neurons are organised in assemblies that have evolved to carry out certain functions. One set specialises in connections to the outside world by which we see, feel, touch, taste and hear; another to our muscles and glands, promoting movement and bodily functions such as digestion and sexual activity; another connects various parts of the brain to itself, enabling us to think, to imagine, to be consciously aware. And all these sets connect with each other to make one person's total, conscious experience.

We are aware of the term 'brain wave'. Scientists are just discovering that short circuits between nerve cells can provide speedier lines of communication through the brain. Evidence of cross-talk emerged in experiments on one region of the brain. When the conventional signalling through synapses was turned off, it was discovered that the nerve cells could still communicate via flows of current between their axons, thread-like extensions used to pass on signals. Moreover, the oscillations of activity were found to be at more than 100 times a second. This type of communication between neurons is faster than the conventional route through synapses by a factor of about ten. The precise function of these high-speed brainwaves has yet to be ascertained but it is already clear that this will shed new light on mental processes such as learning and memory, as well as epilepsy, where there are storms of electrical activity in the brain.

The human brain never stops working and retains the potential for self-renewal throughout life. Every second electrical and chemical impulses keep its user intimately in tune with the rhythms of nature. The circadian rhythms – the biorhythm of the brain – are so familiar as to be taken for granted: our daily sleep and waking patterns; our times of eating and drinking; a woman's monthly cycle and menopause; every individual's ageing cycles. Sometimes when these patterns are disturbed, usually by outward events, we react with unpleasant symptoms. Anyone who has suffered jet lag or experienced SAD – (Seasonal Affective Disorder), a depression caused by lack of sunlight at certain times of the year – has had direct experience of the brain's circadian rhythmicity. Throughout the day there is evidence of cycles of attention and concentration in the brain.

At birth our brain is only 23 per cent of its final adult size. In the first year of life, a baby's brain triples in size to three-quarters of adult size. Rapid growth continues for a further six years after birth, and the whole growing process is not complete until about the 23rd year of life. Cells also start dying from the moment we are born – by the age of 70 our brains will have lost about five per cent of their weight. In comparison, the brain of our nearest relative, the chimpanzee completes its brain growth within twelve months after birth. Much of its brain growth will have taken place before birth.

The brain of a human infant is almost infinitely adaptable. During the first four or five years of life, nerve cells or neurons of the brain are much like the child itself: they are exuberant. Their anatomy is very complex, with more interconnections with other neurons than they can maintain into adulthood. The weakening of these interconnections is being studied with the aim to prolong our ability to learn, recover and extend quality of life. As a result, any disturbance in the brain itself, or in the sensory organs of the eye, ear, or skin, produces a marked response in the infant brain, with new connections formed between previously separate neurons. All of this activity and sensitivity comes to a halt within the first few years of life for humans. After that period, the brain, particularly the massive cerebral cortex which performs all the high-level functions of the brain, is said to be 'hard-wired', a computer term which means permanent. The paths that information signals take in, through and out of the cortex are considered to be fixed at or around the age of five. Teachers can confirm that it is very difficult to undo something that has been incorrectly taught in these early years.

The dominant objective of the many brain and mind institutes around the world is to understand the brain mechanism of the higher functions that characterise human behaviour. They want to understand how we perceive the world around us and later access information we have stored about it. Scientists also look at how we plan and carry out actions upon the external environment, how we attend to one sensory channel to the exclusion of others and how we learn, store, recall, remember and then modify our behaviour in the light of past experience.

Neuroscience is the vast subject that incorporates the fields of systems neuroanatomy, systems neurophysiology, computational neurobiology and cognitive neuropsychology. Mind and brain institutes have adopted an interdisciplinary systems approach to this multifaceted subject of neuroscience. The growth in computer power combined with the interactive feature of the internet has greatly accelerated advancement in this area. Many studies are now being conducted with active, 'cognisant,' human subjects using non-invasive, innocuous methods of imaging and mapping the human brain in action. The results of studies of this type are leading to new understandings of the topography of the brain landscape, of the functions of the healthy brain and of how it is altered by disease or injury. Much of the current work is involved in improving our quality of life. For example, creating advances in rehabilitation medicine, aids for the blind, or for robotic engineering devices that can perform tasks too difficult or dangerous for human workers.

Scientists at the Johns Hopkins University Philip Bard Laboratories of Neurophysiology[17] think that the information needed to record a particular shape or form in the brain is first transmitted by at least one of four types of identified sensory neurons. Work is continuing to identify specifically which type by using research subjects. The subjects touch raised letters of the Braille symbols, and the research team records how the objects are identified by the nervous system. A microelectrode inserted into a single sensory nerve cell axon (transmitting fibre) coming from the fingertip allows the scientist to record every time the cell transmits a signal. By using a computer to convert the 'firings' of many neurons to dots on a chart, the Bard researchers are able to create a visual image of the information being transmitted when a finger touches the object. The results are amazing. For the most part, the neuron-computer-generated image is a striking resemblance of the object itself in miniature, formed by the concurrent firing of hundreds of nerve cells. The object-shaped area of transmissions travels down the entire axons of the nerve cells in this form. Confirming the one sensory neuron type that carries this spatial (existing or happening in space) information may lead to the development of devices that allow blind people to sense 'images' through touch.

The next step in understanding sensory perception is to describe how the spatial information carried by the neurons is recognised in the brain. It is at this point that the concept of pattern recognition becomes important. Pattern recognition is the key to the sensory functions of

---

[17] Johns Hopkins University Philip Bard Laboratories became part of the Zanvyl Krieger Mind/Brain Institute in 1994

the brain and may be the most fundamental element in what is termed 'higher brain function.' Recognition, association, memory and even thinking of objects all begin as pattern recognition. Locating and describing pattern recognition, however, is extremely difficult because the brain collects and assembles a great deal more than the original pattern the sensory organs take in and transmit. Work on aids for the blind is a very interesting area. Surprising to some, one of the most complex and exquisite senses is that of touch. There are 12 kinds of sensory neurons (nerve cells) in the hands and most of them can be mechanically stimulated in some form or another. Some of them respond to vibration and have the properties similar to the nerves involved in hearing. When holding a tool, for example, most people are able to perceive some of the activity at the head or tip of the tool by sensing vibrations. Other types of neurons in the fingers are involved in the ability to sense the three-dimensional form of something touched, much like the sense of vision. This is very interesting. This particular sense of touch has very specifically refined sets of neurons. The skin has two layers of nerve cells scattered throughout, so that when an object is touched, an image of that object is transmitted to certain areas of the brain much as the retina of the eye sends a 'picture' to the visual cortex.

The Bard scientists have begun to understand this seemingly insoluble riddle by demonstrating that the images received by the brain are transformed into altered, abstract forms of representation before they are stored in the brain's memory. After this transformation takes place, the abstract forms are further identified by their comparative relationship with images stored previously in memory. The Bard scientists can verify this process by tracing the form-sensing pathways of neurons from the hand to the brain and discovering what processes are occurring at the synapses (those sites through which one neuron communicates with others using messenger chemicals called neurotransmitters or neuropeptides), or relay stations between the nerve cells, along the way. They are now conducting experiments that allow them literally to follow the physical route by which the touch becomes a memory.

In the computer environment we see our different spoken languages – English, French, Japanese etc., converted to various software 'high-level' languages. For example, ALGOL was written for general applications, COBAL for business applications, FORTRAN for mathematics work, BASIC for general-purpose introductory programming with later derivatives including "C", C+, Unix/XENIX etc. These languages are derived from a 'low-level' machine language, a much more incomprehensible binary code, i.e. a string of '0's and '1's – a pulse of electricity '1' or no pulse '0' (on or off). An internationally accepted code that represents numbers, letters and symbols with unique binary code values, which the computer can manipulate, is known as ASCII (American Standard Code for Information Interchange). For example, when you press the letter '**B**' on a keyboard, the 8-bit (binary digit) code 01000010 (a byte) that represents the digital signal for '**B**', is sent to the computer. The '**?**' symbol is represented by 00111111. This book contains approximately 300KB – 300,000 bytes or characters including spaces. We could store three similar size books comfortably in 1MB of mass storage memory (one million bytes or characters).

We also see in the computer analogy 'conscious', 'unconscious' and 'subconscious' memory. In the computer world, 'conscious' memory is the current process where information is displayed on the screen (VDU). The 'unconscious' memory is the directories and files that reside in the hard disk drive (HDD) awaiting recall. (This information is fixed and is non-volatile – it will remain stored in the hard disk even when the computer 'goes to sleep' or is switched off). The 'subconscious' memory contains the 'operating system', e.g. *Windows XP®*, which is stored in ROM (Read Only Memory) and cannot normally be accessed or changed!

The average capacity of the hard disk drive (HDD) in a Personal Computer today is 10GB and is doubling year on year. Remember a byte is a group of eight bits, which represents coded data. If the data is text then the byte represents a single alphanumeric character, ten bytes represents a single word. One kilobyte (KB) a very short story (1024 bytes), one megabyte (MB) a substantial novel (one million bytes), one gigabyte (GB) a pickup truck filled with paper or a movie at TV quality (one billion bytes or more commonly expressed as 1024 megabytes). Mass storage systems containing terabytes (TB) of data are not uncommon – a terabyte is one trillion bytes or 1024 gigabytes. We even have terms for memory storage that reflect just how much more information we aim to retrieve from our collective minds. For example, the petabyte (PB) 1,000,000,000,000,000 bytes – two petabytes being capable of storing all US academic research libraries – to the exabyte (EB) – 1,000,000,000,000,000,000 bytes. Five exabytes could store all words ever spoken by human beings, to zettabyte (ZB) – 1,000,000,000,000,000,000,000 bytes and yottabyte (YB) – 1,000,000,000,000,000,000,000,000 bytes. It does not seem that long ago when 640KB were considered to be enough for anybody. Today, the average computer at home has the possibility to store 10 billion bytes of data, i.e. 10 billion characters of information which relates to a library of approximately 30,000 books of similar size to this one, in its mass memory storage. This however pales into insignificance compared to our own mass memory storage capacity. It is impossible to compare the two other than to demonstrate how computer memory storage is developing to phenomenal capacities but still some way to go to match the memory capacity in the human brain!

Our everyday world is built upon millions and millions of events, decisions and experiences. In addition to all this we can retrieve memories and information, which we have picked up earlier in our lives, in nanoseconds. Not only this but we can take in a huge amount of data which has been generated by other people, from other spaces and lives. There is so much information available to us today in all forms of media, from books to DVDs. It seems that, unlike computers, we do not run out of memory or the ability to take in information, although the process may slow down as we age.

It is very straightforward to backup data on our computer. How do we back-up *our* information? Is this the purpose of sleep perhaps? We can delete files from the computer memory but it seems impossible to erase information once established in our human memory, even those most unwanted memories! Incidentally, we are also similar to the computer in that we would be totally useless without memory!

A simple example to illustrate the size and complexity of our memory and memory recall can be demonstrated with an experiment on London taxi drivers.[18] These taxi drivers have shown neuroscientists that part of the brain called the right hippocampus is crucial for navigating. Brain scanner tests on cabbies have shown where the ability to remember the route to a destination resides. A network of brain regions may support the construction of a mental map of space, but only the right hippocampus is specifically involved in relating the elements of a route together in an overall framework for navigation. The study, conducted with Professor Richard Frackowiak and Professor Chris Frith, shows that the right hippocampus is activated in the brain when drivers recall complicated routes, but not during other types of complex memory recall. When, for example, the cabbies remembered information about landmarks they activated brain regions including the occipitotemporal regions, posterior cingulate gyrus, medial parietal area and parahippocampal gyrus. The route memory test also triggered activation in these brain areas. However, the right hippocampus was activated only during the route memory test. The discovery helps to open the study of human navigation and suggests that different brain network support different types of memory. In the study, the researchers analysed navigation by imaging the brains of the taxi drivers with positron emission tomography, which highlights activity in the brain by measuring changes in blood flow. The study indicated that the right hippocampus was activated significantly when they recalled complicated routes, but not during other types of memory recall. It was not activated when they were

---

[18] Conducted by Dr Eleanor Maguire of London's Institute of Neurology in 1997

asked to recall the plots of popular films – a test also requiring the recall of information involving a sequence of events. London taxi drivers have to train for several years to acquire 'the knowledge' and gain a licence. This example also highlights the complexity of different types of memory in our brain and how an adult brain, once thought incapable of re-growth, can expand new regions that are in constant demand.

Some individuals have good memory access, others have poor memory access and find it difficult to concentrate and there are those with exceptional 'photographic' memory. Self-proclaimed memory experts have made fortunes, marketing and selling their programmes which claim will improve memory or address why a memory can be bad. All these schemes promise rapid results, using simple techniques. *The Mind Map Book*[19] gives an excellent modern analysis of the human brain and explains how those brains historically considered to be 'great' used a brain-based mode of advanced thought: Radiant Thinking and its natural expression, Mind Mapping. The book describes these multi-dimensional thinking techniques that distinguish between mental storage *capacity* and mental storage *efficiency* that is available to everyone but lies dormant in 95 per cent of the population.

As previously explained, memory is a key component to the 'intelligence' of the computer system. We talk about computers having 8MB, 16MB, 32MB, 64MB, 128MB etc., of RAM; 1.2GB, 2.2GB, 4.5GB, 9.4GB, 18GB, 36GB, 72GB........1.5TB onwards and upwards non-volatile mass storage memory capacity,

---

[19] Tony Buzan *The Mind Map Book* Published by BBC Books 1993

where information is stored in Hard Disk Drive(s) and remains even when the power is switched off. The more memory a system has, the more data it holds and the more powerful it is. We also hear the term 'redundancy' associated with memory. This 'redundant' memory is additional or duplicate memory that enables operations to continue following a failure of part of the memory in a computer system. Other areas of memory in the computer include cache memory; this is a dedicated portion of a computer Random Access Memory (RAM) that stores the last items that were retrieved from a disk. In certain applications the cache can significantly improve performance.

Like the computer, we have different types and layers of memory. Our layers of memory have been accumulated during what has happened and what is about to happen in our present life together with the memories of our ancestors going all the way back in time to when life first began on Earth. But in the context of the *Alien Visitor* gene theory, we have also gained the *Alien Visitor* memory of its life on Earth together with its own history going back to when the *Alien Visitor's* life first evolved on some distant planet!

It is interesting when you continue this computer memory analogy to the human brain when we die. When a computer "dies" and is replaced with a new one, we can either transfer the data over to the new computer's hard disk drive (HDD) via USB pen drives, floppy disks, back-up tapes, CD's, Wi-Fi, across the internet, etc., or we can delete or forget about it. Or we can add this old drive to the new system by attaching it as a slave or secondary drive to the new master or primary drive. This means that the new computer can access the historical data from the old computer in D: (or D: and E: etc., if the drive had been partitioned) on the new computer, with C: being the new primary drive. I believe that this analogy applies to the human brain where information is passed on from the older generation to the new not through magnetic storage memory devices as in the case of the computer, but through our memory genes. I also believe that a great deal of our history has survived in the collective memories of the people who exist on our planet today.

Through this computer memory analogy we could also explore the possibility that when we die, our mind, (our memory, our soul) is transported to another place, another dimension. Had the *Alien Visitor* devised a means of collating the data that each and every one of us has collected during our moment on Earth? So death may not be final, but a prelude to other experiences?

Mind games – such as chess – exercise the mind through the development of the memory. It is interesting that humans are the only creatures on Earth to play intricate mind games for fun. Perhaps these games came about after the *Alien Visitor* bred with our ancestors, boosting the capacity of early human brains and the desire to use them. The earliest writings of ancient civilisations refer to games similar in concept to tic-tac-toe (noughts and crosses). Something like draughts was played in Egypt. A Greek vase – thought to be around 2,500 years old – depicts Ajax and Achilles playing a form of backgammon. Chess is said to have originated in India around 600 AD under the name 'Chaturanga', a word describing the four traditional army units of Indian military forces: foot soldiers (pawns), cavalry (knights), chariots (rooks), and elephants (today's bishops). Since the 1970s, however, more and more weight has been given to the idea that China already had a version of chess before India. There were mentions of Xiangqi (Chinese chess) in documents during the Warring States period (403-221 BC). Confucius is said to have known Go (a game referred to in Chinese texts of about 1000 BC). To Plato, games were a vital part of a leader's training. Board games have been portrayed by artists through the centuries, from ancient Greece and Rome to the illuminated manuscripts of medieval monks and the modern art of Ernst and Duchamp. To all of them, the games had a mystical significance.

Today, the number of games played is expanding rapidly and within the last ten years there has been an explosion in games to be played on computers or televisions. Sport has also experienced a rapid worldwide growth as can be seen from the ever-increasing number of events that are now included in the Olympic Games. Mental toughness training is now a prerequisite to serious sports men and women to improve their concentration and self-belief. Some methods actually play out the potential critical situation before it happens, so that if it does happen, then the individual is mentally prepared. Examples of this are putting on the 18th green to win the golf championship or taking a penalty in injury time to win the soccer game. I think all these games express a desire to challenge the mind and uncover mental skills.

We can see a human mind at work which is superior to other creatures on Earth. Just how superior we are will be investigated in the next chapter.

Chapter 8

GENIUS ONE AND ALL

I think all humans possess the *Alien Visitor* gene and, as I have said earlier, *Homo sapiens* missing this gene are not humans but something like the Yeti or Big Foot. As all humans have the gene, I believe they therefore have an incredible intelligence. Obviously, there are different levels and kinds of intellect. People we recognise as geniuses – whether it be in the field of mathematics, the arts or football – are those who come closest to the original intelligence possessed by the *Alien Visitor*. Some of us are able to access this knowledge and make the most of it while others, for a number of factors, do not have the opportunities to focus on their potential. But I am in no doubt; every person does possess this extra-terrestrial intelligence and potential for genius.

It seems impossible to believe that any human could share an intelligence equal to that of the *Alien Visitor* which – as I have argued earlier – was a much more advanced life-form than us. But all through our history we do have examples of people who seem to have an intelligence far beyond that of most people. It is frequently these people who change the world because they are able to come up with an invention or idea beyond the reach of most others. I think that for reasons that are as yet unknown some people are geniuses while the full potential in the rest of us is hidden to some extent.

I would like to look at some examples of geniuses and unusual aspects of their lives, which might explain how they have been able to make the most of their intelligence.

Parents or teachers are sometimes able to recognise the potential in their own children, when ironically, they may not see it in themselves. There are examples of geniuses who seem to have benefited from the nurturing of their intelligence. Two illustrations are the philosopher Nostradamus and composer Mozart. Many of Nostradamus' maternal and paternal ancestors were skilled mathematicians and doctors, which perhaps gave them the ability to recognise the same capacity to learn in the young Nostradamus. Or maybe they placed a lot of importance on drawing out intellectual potential. He was informally educated by his grandfather, a doctor and master of the celestial science of astrology and subsequently studied humanities at Avignon and the theory of medicine and philosophy at Montpellier, the most famous medical school in France. Mozart is recognised as one of the world's greatest composers. At three years old he was picking out chords on the harpsichord, at four playing short pieces, at five was composing. There are anecdotes about his precise memory of pitch and about his scribbling a concerto at the age of five. Just before he was six, his father took him to Munich to play at the Bavarian court and a few months later they went to Vienna and were heard at the imperial court and in noble houses. Leopold Mozart was very keen to develop his son's talent and make it known to the world. In fact he called Mozart 'the miracle which God let be born in Salzburg' and spoke of how he felt he had a duty to draw 'the miracle' to the notice of the world. He was certainly a parent who worked hard to draw the genius from his son and make it apparent to all. Incidentally, he also nurtured the musical gift of his daughter Nannerl, Mozart's sister, who was also an extremely good musician but is possibly lesser known because the people which society recognises as geniuses are frequently, if not always, men and particularly in seventeenth and eighteenth century Europe. Perhaps Leopold's ability to quickly spot his children's musical gifts came from his own musical background. He was the author of a well-known violin tutor book. The British scientist, Francis Galton, is believed to have published the first evidence that genius runs in families in his work Hereditary Genius in 1869. My explanation for this is that we all possess the *Alien Visitor* gene so every member of every family has the capacity for genius. Perhaps it is seen to run in some families because somewhere, one of the members has recognised its own potential and attempts to draw it out of its children and this is in turn may be passed down the line. It is also likely that high self-esteem was encouraged in these families!

Another way in which an individual's genius seems to become apparent is through the suffering of certain disorders. We do not really know why children or adults who suffer physical or mental difficulties in one area should seem to be so over-compensated in another but we do have examples of this. One of the most famous is the physicist Albert Einstein who, according to *Einstein a Life*[20] was born with a swollen, misshapen head and overweight body. Within months everything had become

---

[20] Denis Brian *Einstein a Life* Published by John Wiley & Sons Ltd 1996

normal, except for the back of Einstein's skull. That always remained unusually angular. But for his parents the worrying was not over because Einstein's speech was late in developing. It seemed he had a form of autism characterised by abnormal self-absorption, a lack of response to people and actions and limited ability to communicate. There is some dispute as to when Einstein began to speak, but he was a late and reluctant talker. He was quiet and withdrawn in the company of strangers but his younger sister was the victim of his wild temper. Einstein's face would turn yellow before a rage. However, he started to show his intelligence when he was five and his father gave him a magnetic compass and this appeared to trigger his mind. What followed, of course, was a major contribution to our understanding of the laws of science. There are many cases of people with autism who possess a number of extraordinary skills, which first develop in childhood. It seems these children can directly tap into areas of the brain and perform tasks – such as drawing or solving mathematical problems – which people who are not autistic may never be able to do even if they have been taught and carried out repetitive exercises.

A recent example that demonstrates these skills involves the artist Stephen Wiltshire who was diagnosed autistic when he was three. From a young age he demonstrated an extraordinary talent from drawing from memory which he still possesses. In 2005 at the age of 33 he depicted Tokyo on a 10 metre long and 2 metre wide canvas within seven days after a short helicopter ride over the city. The amazing detail and sense of perspective of this panoramic drawing is described as faultless.

From time to time we get glimpses of amazing capabilities inside a human brain which lends great credence to my "alien visitor gene theory".

The Italian criminologist, Cesare Lombroso, is among those who believe geniuses belong to a separate psychobiological species (in terms of their biological functions and structures), differing as much from ordinary man in his mental and emotional processes as man differs from the ape. My contention is that the genius is not a function of a different species but the hidden part of any human which is hard to access. It is the concentration of our intelligence that separates us from the ape. Some disorders seem to enable their sufferers to take a short cut to using parts of the brain that carry out complicated operations. We do not yet know why this is. Perhaps it is these people who have ultimately made us aware of the potential within all of us because they show us what we can be capable of. Maybe it is their achievements, which have prompted us to nurture talents in others, knowing what the human is capable of.

Many geniuses, particularly those from the arts, attribute their best works to the influence of drugs. In fact, some of the English Romantics – mainly Byron, Coleridge and Shelley – are almost as well-known for their drug-taking as their poetry. They were so convinced that narcotics stimulated their imagination that they purposely took drugs together before sitting down to write. According to two French academics, Tigranne Hadengue and Hugo Verlomme – in *The Book of Cannabis* – Alexandre Dumas used drugs while writing *The Three Musketeers*. In *The Count of Monte Cristo* it seems Dumas refers to his drug-taking himself when he writes: "The world is grateful to the merchant of happiness" which has been taken by some academics as a reference to nineteenth century drug dealers. Another French writer, Honoré de Balzac – who is studied as one of the proponents of a style of writing known as realism – also seems to have used drugs to write his novels. In a letter in 1845, he told Ewelina Hanska, who was to become his wife: "My mind is so powerful; I needed a more powerful dose. I heard celestial voices and saw divine paintings." Research has shown us that all drugs act through the brain's neurotransmitters and alter behaviour. Caffeine in tea, coffee and chocolate counteracts adenosine, an inhibitory chemical. It stimulates the heart and raises blood pressure. Amphetamines stimulate the release of dopamine, affecting the brain's 'reward' centre. Prolonged use can lead to paranoia, even psychosis. Ecstasy and Prozac induce euphoria by producing serotonin, making more of it available to the receptors. There are, of course, obvious side effects. Prolonged use can permanently damage serotonin pathways, causing irreversible damage to the working memory and depression. Coleridge's addiction to opium is believed to have caused the nightmares he describes.

Perhaps we will learn more about the effects of drugs on the creative processes of the mind and memory, as drugs are developed to treat the brain. Most of these drugs today are being invented in an attempt to treat Alzheimer's disease. The first drug to enhance memory, Tacrine, was granted a licence for the treatment in America at the beginning of 1997. Its effects seem to be quite limited but it has inspired another generation of drugs, which will be tested within the next five years and are likely to be more effective. Drug companies have been attempting to develop cognitive enhancers, the so-called 'smart drugs', for many years. They increase blood flow to the brain, improve oxygen and glucose uptake and increase the availability of neurotransmitters. In addition, more than 200 chemicals are being investigated, using supercomputers, in the race to find an effective treatment for Alzheimer's disease. Recent studies suggest that the key to memory enhancement is reinforcing brain synapses-junctions across which nerve cells communicate. A new family of drugs called ampakines increases the sensitivity of the synapses, easing the flow of electrical impulses between nerve cells. Ampakines can help rats to remember the way round a maze and are also on trial in America for Alzheimer's disease. There is another drug being developed to ward off age-related memory loss and combat the early symptoms of Alzheimer's disease which may also lead to treatment for children born with genetic learning difficulties. It raises the possibility of having a treatment that would erase parts of long-term memory relating to specific unhappy experiences. Some of the research into these treatments has shown even young men with normal memories perform up to 20 per cent better in tests of short-term recall, improving their capacity to learn. Drug companies, testing the 'smart drugs', have reported improvements to concentration, memory and problem-solving abilities among test groups. They are also reported to have improved reaction times and short-term memory in healthy people. In the future we may gain a lot of knowledge about how chemicals can be used to improve intelligence and memory. At the moment this work is focused on treating Alzheimer's but perhaps a spin-off from this will be the creation of drugs, which could help us tap into the higher functions of our brains. Another way in which we may be able to access these capabilities in the future is through the use of computers. There are already several methods of obtaining information about what the brain is doing at a particular time. The most promising is by taking electroencephalograms or EEGs.

These are obtained by using electrodes placed on the scalp to detect the electrical activity. In theory, it should be possible to apply the electrodes while a subject is listening to music and find out from the EEG signals which types of activity in the brain are triggered by the music. In practice this is incredibly difficult, since the brain is never working exclusively on processing music. Although taking the average of many EEG recordings can help, the complexity of the brainwave means that finding recurring patterns with musical thoughts is like looking for needles in haystacks. Evidence suggesting the brain processes music and language in a similar way has allowed researchers of both disciplines to profit from each other's findings. There is a chance that by comparing these brain signals with the structure of the music – which the subject is listening to – patterns may be found. This could give clues on how to relate brainwaves to music. Pattern- matching technology on a type of computer called a neural network could be used. In the future this research could allow people to play instruments and writing scores using their brain activity alone. This opens up a world of possibilities presently only available to those with years of musical training.

Another trigger for genius is body chemistry. People who suffer grief or stress seem to suddenly be able to produce their best work. Many of Keats' poems were composed following the deaths of his family members. The former Beatle, Paul McCartney said in an interview[21] that he suddenly found himself writing *Yesterday* while suffering grief following a family death. Perhaps the creative process is improved by the way the body reacts when encountering problems, which it does not have to deal with every day. We often hear of people who are not recognised as geniuses until after their deaths and their lives seem to have been filled with stress brought on by poverty and exclusion. Perhaps it is, ironically, this stress that alters their body chemistry, compelling them to create the work we later recognise as that of a genius. Some modern psychoanalytic theories suggest that genius – like neurosis and psychosis – has its source in basic conflict between the self and environment; in the genius these conflicts are resolved in such a way that the symptoms and products are socially useful and valued. There are people – particularly those of strict religious orders – who attempt to change the balance of their bodies by imposing stress on themselves, such as fasting or keeping a vow of silence. There are accounts of people being able to perform superhuman feats after imposing these regimes on themselves. Some can walk on hot coals. There are reports of people who say they experience a heightening of their senses to the point where they can hear dust falling to the ground. Probably the most famous example is Jesus who crosses a desert despite fasting for forty days and nights. There are many types of therapies – such as acupuncture or reflexology – which are thousands of years old and attempt to release the body's maximum potential by unblocking the energy or meridian lines in the body. I have already discussed how medical advances

---

[21] *Parkinson* BBC1 1999

made by drug companies could help us find out how to use our brains to their full capacity but perhaps there are also answers in the ancient natural therapies. The medical profession is being encouraged to study how complementary medicines and therapies can be used to treat chronic conditions for which conventional medicine is frequently ineffective. Nearly 40 per cent of GPs in Britain are prescribing some kind of alternative treatment for their patients. Maybe research and a greater use of these therapies will point to ways of boosting our mental skills.

Intensive exercise – such as that performed by top athletes in training – can also be seen as a factor in creating genius. Runners are able to achieve speeds that far exceed those of people who do not exercise. The 100 m champion, Linford Christie, can run the distance in under ten seconds – a feat which most of us only dream of. In some religious philosophies – such as Gnosticism – there is a belief that exercise is necessary in order to achieve our full potential and that a lack of exercise could leave us in a state where we never experience our full range of emotions and understanding. Some academics believe the hymn *Lord of the Dance* actually refers to these exercises.

It may sound far-fetched, but alien abductions could also offer an explanation for genius. Alien abductions are constantly being reported. Many 'abductees' give accounts which have much in common which each other. They describe a sense of 'lost time' after witnessing a UFO. Some later go on to describe 'flashbacks' which they feel relate to events that have taken place during that 'lost time'. Some find these 'flashbacks', or the whole abduction experience, have heightened their intelligence in a variety of fields. Alien abductions may help to 'stimulate' access to a 'hidden' knowledge which we have inherited from our *Alien Visitor* ancestors but is difficult for us to retrieve from our memories. This could give an explanation for why similar inventions are made at the same time but by people living in different countries and cultures who have no connection with each other.

We do not know why some people have unlocked their genius and others have not. Obviously, many geniuses live with a combination of the factors I have listed rather than just one. For example, Einstein suffered with illness and in addition spent great periods of time under stress as he worked. It is probably not the case that a regular intake of drugs can bring about genius. Drug-taking in itself is often an activity performed by an already troubled or grieving body which is probably going through a multitude of reactions before a drug is introduced. In the case of the Romantics, the drug-taking was an activity they indulged in while sharing their ideas and reading their work aloud to each other. It seems impossible to attribute their work solely to their use of drugs, as their nurturing of each other's ideas is also an important factor. Perhaps one common thing in many of the geniuses I have listed is that within their lifetimes they lived in unusual circumstances or under unusual pressures that may have altered the way they responded to or felt they fitted into the world. Perhaps this accounts for their different perspectives. I am sure there are many other factors that account for genius that we do not yet comprehend. Until there is more research into the way chemicals work in the body, it is not possible to be specific about the effects of disorders, stress, drugs and exercise on a body or how they channel genius.

It is possible that we all display intelligence gained from the *Alien Visitor* because every human outstrips the capabilities of our nearest ancestors in the animal world. But the reason I think we have some geniuses is because they have found ways of making more of the *Alien Visitor* gene or genes which we all have. Either by nurturing of expressions of intelligence or creativity or by shifts in body chemistry they are able to draw out their *Alien Visitor* gene or genes and perhaps suppress other aspects of human life which can stifle the possibilities offered by our heritage from the *Alien Visitor*.

We all believe that genius is only bestowed on a few people. Even Collins' *English Dictionary* defines a genius a one with "exceptional ability of a highly original kind." It was not until the seventeenth century that the word 'genius' assumed its modern meaning. However, we do class people such as Aristotle or Plato as geniuses today, so, from our point of view, there have probably always been geniuses but it is not clear how they were regarded by their contemporaries. Although we have a definition of genius it is based on the observation of these people and comparison of them with the majority rather than explanation of why they are geniuses. However, my contention is that we all have the potential to be geniuses but the reason we perceive them as 'exceptional' and 'original' is because only a handful of people live up to this potential.

We are intrigued by genius and have many ways of analysing it. A large chunk of any government's work is to educate and raise the intelligence of its people because education is something most people rate as the most important quality to have and an issue on which they would vote. Ironically, in attempts to define genius or intelligence we sideline many talents, jobs and points of view as not intelligent. In most societies in the modern world, the person with a doubtful command of mathematics and a first language is perceived as being unlikely to crack quantum mechanics or write a major literary work and therefore as not being intelligent or possessing any capacity to attain genius. Much of what we perceive as intelligence is defined according to attempts to structure our societies in a certain way. However, if we place a group of people in a different society, we might re-evaluate their intelligence. In James M. Barrie's book, *The Admirable Crichton,* a butler is marooned on a desert island with his masters. The butler has a number of invaluable practical skills that enable him to become viewed as the leader on the island. However, the party is rescued by a passing ship and when they return to their own society, the butler continues to serve his masters as before. This example shows definitions of intelligence – which are commonly held by a society – are those which benefit those particular societies and cannot be seen as absolute. Obviously, a butler using his skills in a desperate situation is not an example of genius. However, this example shows that within that desert island society the butler at least had a chance of having his talents more valued and nurtured with the possibility that he would be encouraged to reach his potential. As a butler in his own society he is required to perform the same tasks over and over at the bidding of other people. They probably have little interest in his development as an individual because that would conflict with their need to have repetitive tasks carried out for them.

There is also the problem that our own methods of measuring intelligence seem to fall short of explaining genius. A high IQ is thought to guarantee genius, but this measurement cannot be used to calculate the genius of many athletes where a physical rather than mental brilliance is required. IQ tests identify academic abilities. In the jargon of the IQ testers, academically brilliant people have a higher 'g' rating. 'g' is the unit used to define the quantity of intelligence. It was invented by Charles Spearman, the English psychologist. According to IQ testers, you cannot acquire more 'g' during a lifetime but are born with a fixed quotient. I believe this system of measuring our intelligence fails to take into account our hidden potential, which may become channeled, in later life. I agree with the IQ testers that our intelligence is hard-wired into us from birth but my contention is that the individual's full intelligence is not always on display from the start and needs to be unlocked. There are also many people who never take IQ tests, leading to assumptions that few people have high IQs, but is this assumption based on enough research?

The difficulty with social nurturing of intelligence is that the system only accepts those who show what society decides is a sign of intelligence. In much of the modern world this is having a high IQ and passing exams at school. Once educated, these people are likely to be best nurtured and rewarded with jobs which ask them to use their imagination and develop their own skills, at least some of the time. All companies employ people who they believe suit their 'culture'. People who do not go through this system very often find themselves in jobs where they are not asked to develop themselves because, as the butler in the example above, they are needed to carry out repetitive tasks. There is almost always a social structure based on its concept of intelligence. In some ways this is even more unfair than a hierarchy based on birth because it withdraws the opportunities from individuals to develop their own talents and explore their intelligence that comes from the *Alien Visitor* gene, they have the same as everyone else. At its worst, the people who hold up a social definition of intelligence can persecute and isolate a person – who is later recognised as a genius – for not being intelligent. There are lots of examples of people we hold as geniuses today, who struggled to gain notice in their own lives and lived in terrible poverty, such as the painter Vincent Van Gogh. I think this proves that a social context determines perceptions of intelligence and it is only when a person is regarded by a different or later society that his talent is seen because the same social prejudices do not apply.

We are unable to explain why individuals produce novels, plays, poetry, stories, jokes, cartoons, music, sculpture, painting, or scientific theories when the majority of the human race cannot. The pitfalls for the development of genius are many. If, for example, a potentially great inventor happened to be born into the caste system and live in a remote, impoverished village in India, he would be less likely to be able to achieve his invention than if he were being nurtured at Cambridge University and had access to laboratories and other people with whom he could develop his ideas.

One of the hardest questions for me to answer is why we have cases of two children from the same family who develop in very different ways – one may learn how to stretch itself and perhaps even become a genius while the other does not. The difficulty arises because it seems that both children have the *Alien Visitor* gene and the same upbringing so it seems, on the face of it, that both children should either enjoy the nurturing of their potential or not, depending on the parents. The problem is that there are different ways of expressing intelligence. While the parents may recognise it in one child and be able to nurture it – perhaps because they share the same kind of intelligence – they may not see it or know how to draw it out in the other child. But my theory is that we do all have this intelligence which, when fully understood, can produce genius. Once we accept this, we know our task is to look for it in other people rather than dismissing them as not having intelligence or worth. A study of more than 6,500 children – published in the *Archives of Diseases in Childhood* – found that children who grow up in homes where there are a number of problems are twice as likely to be below average height by the time they are seven than children who grow up in happier environments. The study found differences of around 13 centimetres (five inches) between the shortest and the tallest children studied. It concluded that great stress was capable of slowing the production of the growth hormone. This shows children can be physically stunted by a lack of nurturing. It is possible that this lack of physical growth can accompany a lack of growth of their intelligence and skills.

Although it is obviously interesting to analyze genius – as I am doing in this chapter – I believe there is another way in which we can comprehend it and that is by recognising it in ourselves as our inheritance from the *Alien Visitor.*

My proof that we all share this potential is that we often recognise in others or ourselves what we call 'flashes of genius' – capabilities which seem to stretch beyond those normally achieved. When John Milton described writing his epic poem *Paradise Lost,* he said the idea came to him in his sleep and somehow Milton was able to find a way of letting the poetry flow out of him. Milton described the process as a visitation by a mysterious spirit whom he called the "heavenly muse" who dictated the poem to him at night, while he was asleep, in snatches of 30 lines or so. When he woke up, he would call for a copyist (he had himself been blind for some ten years by this time) to take the lines down. His 'muse', he claimed, was the identical spirit who had dictated the Book of Genesis to Moses and this meant that *Paradise Lost* was no mere human invention but as authoritative as the Bible. It seems Milton believed the poem came out of a part of his mind he did not usually access but he was somehow, suddenly, able to use.

Secondly, there does seem to be an expanding number of people demonstrating talents that would have been viewed as unusual in earlier times. For example, large numbers of today's musicians have achieved the kinds of performances that would have been rarer in Mozart's time. There are many amateur athletes who have run marathon times for which Olympic gold medals were awarded early in the twentieth century. Reaching the summit of Mount Everest is now commonplace – as many as 30 climbers on a given day. In schools, a higher number of girls are seen to be achieving good grades in all subjects. There are probably a huge number of factors, which have brought these changes about, but most of them must come from a desire in individuals to stretch themselves and a tolerance in societies which allows for the nurturing of more talents.

Thirdly, we all have the instinctive ability to recognise genius. People who have never studied music or painting will find themselves humming Mozart's 'Eine Kleine Nachtmusik', or pausing before the 'Mona Lisa' but do not do this with every piece of music or painting they come across. There is something about genius that we respond to even though we do not know why. Many philosophers struggle to define what is genius or quality or why we have these reactions. I think we react because we get a sudden glimpse into what we might all be able to achieve. We call people geniuses even though we know little or nothing about their positions in their societies. There are people such as Leonardo da Vinci of whom we know virtually nothing, but we still hail him as a genius. It is thought he was born the illegitimate child of Ser Piero da Vinci, a 25-year-old notary from Vinci. But there are conflicting ideas about his mother ranging from reports that she was a young woman called Caterina, of uncertain surname and the daughter of a woodsman to someone with close ties to the church and of higher birth. The authenticity of birth certificates believed to be his is uncertain.

I do not think it is just high art which can provoke this feeling that we have witnessed genius at work. We feel awe when we look upon the Sphinx or pyramids in Egypt and we are intrigued – although we do not know why – by these objects. Evidence of this is their frequent use in films. Perhaps when we see these objects, we do not just recognise the work of genius, or *Alien Visitor* intelligence, but they also set off a very hidden memory, contained in our *Alien Visitor* gene. There may be some time in the future when we will be able to piece together these fragments of hidden memory, which occasionally surface. Maybe we will also find techniques allowing us to choose to use this memory rather than waiting for a flash of memory to happen to us. Some philosophers – such as Jung – suggest focusing on the objects, which prompt these odd memories in order that we uncover our hidden memories. He warns against becoming too involved in our daily lives, leaving us little time to ponder on these memories. I personally think that my daily drive past Silbury Hill has channeled my thoughts to produce this theory.

Chapter 9

THE GENE IS OUT OF THE BOTTLE

Scientists across the world are trying to come up with a blueprint of human DNA that will allow them to create a human on paper, explaining how the body is built and maintained. Perhaps when we have this we will be able to identify an *Alien Visitor* gene.

Arguably, the most important scientific breakthrough in the twentieth century was the deciphering of the double helix chain-like molecular structure of DNA or deoxyribonucleic acid – found in every form of life – at Cambridge in 1953 by Dr James Watson and Dr Francis Crick. Genes are the sections of DNA, which tell the rest of the cell how to make amino acids. These are then joined into chains of up to 100,000 units to make proteins. Once a protein has been built it folds into a characteristic shape and goes to work. Proteins are the most vital chemical complexes in our bodies. They are used everywhere to make cell walls, carry messages (called neuropeptides) and to produce reactions. Every cell of a given creature contains an identical set of genes. What makes the cells behave differently – for example as skin cells rather than liver cells – depends on which genes are dormant and which are switched on. Each gene is its own microcomputer and evolution is changing that tiny microprocessor.

In 1999, scientists at The Sanger Centre in Cambridge announced they had cracked the genetic code for the human body, but in fact they have decoded only the part of the body which is richest in genes. Along with scientists in America and Japan, they are racing to produce the entire human genetic code - known as the *Human Genome Project*. Their discoveries will revolutionise medicine in the future and it is important that all discoveries remain in the public domain so they could be shared on the internet and can quickly be turned into medical treatments. The task of understanding a complete DNA sequence seems very difficult as scientists are studying billions of single cells and investigating genes using measurements such as nanometres where one nanometre = 1/1,000,000,000 metre. The scientists are putting some of their findings onto a website to create a massive database and are pooling their findings. When the DNA sequence for a human has been fully deciphered and interpreted, we will have the technology to analyse our genes and keep them on file. Every detail of the body chemistry that predisposes us to diseases could be traceable. Doctors will be able to quickly spot a cystic fibrosis carrier or a woman at high risk of inherited breast cancer as well as accurately predict future medical problems for the patient. Scientists might be able to eliminate diseases. Perhaps chemists will be able to take the personal gene profiles and create medicine tailored to individuals, which could be taken to correct hereditary problems.

There is a steady flow of announcements of the discovery of genes that are thought to be responsible for many conditions. Scientists have found genes linked to high blood pressure and suggested ways inherited deafness could be corrected.   There have been breakthroughs in gene therapy to treat both muscular dystrophy and haemophilia. Researchers are working on revolutionary treatments for Alzheimer's and certain forms of cancer. There is also pioneering work to find ways of changing the brain's chemistry – by introducing genes – in order to cure paralysing brain diseases such as Canavan disease. Scientists are looking to see if top athletes have genes which enable them to move faster than other people. Attempts are being made to isolate genes that cause shyness, baldness or trigger the ageing process. There is much controversy about attempts at cloning genes. The genetically modified food industry is already advanced enough to attract scrutiny and foods are for sale. Scientists at the Roslin Institute in Edinburgh gained worldwide fame when they created a sheep called Dolly using nuclear replacement. Other work in the field of genetics could eventually enable us to understand which chemical reactions within the body give rise to our emotions, actions and behaviour.

The rapid development of DNA technology is now being used to give a more accurate account of the movements and identity of our early ancestors. For example, there is an international effort to identify genes that can distinguish between the different waves of Stone Age immigrants spreading from Africa and the Middle East across Europe.

The first genetic map of the British Isles has revealed that we are united by common DNA. The Institute of Molecular Medicine at Oxford University has profiled 6,000 people and by comparing their blood samples with DNA extracted from the remains of Stone Age people. They discovered that 99 per cent could trace their origins directly back to the Britons who populated the fertile wooded valleys carved out by Ice Age glaciers when Britain was still joined to the European mainland. Anybody who knows that their maternal grandmother was born in the British Isles is almost certain to be genetically identical to a Palaeolithic ancestor through a family chain untouched by more recent races such as the Celts, who are thought to have arrived in Britain in 700 BC, from mainland Europe. The project is examining genes from structures called mitochondria, responsible for programming activity within individual cells. This DNA is inherited solely through the maternal line which suggests that the male invaders played a small role in our genetic make-up. Specific genes and their mutations have been compared to DNA derived from about 20 ancient skeletons from Britain and the Continent.

So far DNA technology has not been used to look for this *Alien Visitor* gene but if we wanted to search for it there are many mummies from the early civilisations that might hold this information. The Egyptians are best known for mummifying their dead but this practice has been found on every continent on Earth. There are numerous examples of cultures involved in mummification from as far afield as the sophisticated fishing tribe called the Chinchoros who lived on the north coast of what is now Chile, who were embalming their dead as early as 5000 BC. Further north another coastal group at Paloma were mummifying their dead as early as 4000 BC and 5,000 years later, during the time of the Inca (approximately 1100 to 1500 AD), the Andean tradition of preserving the dead was still intact. Unfortunately, when the Spanish conquered the Inca in the sixteenth and seventeenth centuries, they destroyed countless Incan burial sites – partly for religious reasons, but also to plunder the gold often buried with mummies. As a result, few Incan burial sited remain. The Aleut people who lived on the Aleutian Islands off the coast of Alaska, the people of Papua, New Guinea, the Anasazi who lived in the American Southwest and the Caucasian people from the remote Chinese desert region known as the Takla Makan are further examples. Interestingly, the perfectly preserved mummies from the remote Chinese desert region known as the Takla Makan had long reddish-blond hair with blue eyes and over two metres (six feet) tall; tartan clad with Caucasian heritage (European features) and did not appear to be the ancestors of modern-day Chinese people. Archaeologists now think they may have been the citizens of an ancient civilisation that existed at the crossroads between China and Europe. The Chachapoyas, or Cloud People who were Peruvian contemporaries of the Incas, are a further example of a lost tribe of tall white people with blond hair and blue eyes and who remarkably appear to share the same ideas and beliefs – mummification, similar symbols and forms of writing etc. But the mummies who could shed the most light on our history are those of the Guanches. The Guanches are the mysterious natives of the Canary Islands. They were almost exterminated by the Spaniards when they invaded the archipelago at the turn of the fifteenth century. Tall, with a brown complexion, blue or grey eyes and blondish hair, the Guanches have long intrigued the anthropologists. Isolated on their islands, the Guanches were prevented, until the advent of the Spanish, from sexually mingling with other races. So, they preserved their pristine Cro-Magnon genetic traits in a more or less pure fashion until that date. Today, the blond, blue-eyed, tall stock has tended to disappear from the population but there still remain a few individuals known as 'recessives'. Furthermore, the Guanches mummified their dead and this material can be studied by researchers, particularly concerning traits such as blood type and racial characteristics. This strange mode of disposing of the dead – which the Guanches shared with the Polynesians, the Egyptians and the Mayas – has been mooted by several authorities as indicating a close affinity among these distant nations. I believe that through the development of DNA technology, we can show clear links from the mummified remains of the Guanche, Celtic, Peruvian, Egyptian mummies to a single origin – the *Alien Visitor.*

For example, geneticists are investigating genetic anomalies resulting from Marfan's Syndrome, which is believed to be a disorder among Egyptian pharaohs that resulted in extremely tall odd-looking individuals with long fingers and faces and narrow eyes. The many paintings of the pharaoh Akhenaten exhibit an almost complete expression of this genetic mutation. It should be of no surprise to find significant genetic anomalies in the early *Alien Visitor* and *Homo sapiens* hybrid offspring. But the main point here being if these pharaohs were some of the early descendants of the *Alien Visitor*, then those today suffering from this syndrome can be seen to be closely connected genetically to the early *Alien Visitor* offspring. It is interesting to note that Abraham Lincoln, Rachmaninoff, Niccolò Paganini and Mary Queen of Scots are among those though to have had Marfan's Syndrome.

Perhaps mummification was a process first practised by the *Alien Visitor* as a way of preserving a body with the intention of bringing it back to life at later date. Or maybe the *Alien Visitor* preserved the bodies as specimens for scientific work. Maybe the visitor wanted to provide a genetic database for future generations of its own race or the race it left on Earth to analyse. I hope that DNA samples from our *Homo* ancestors – who lived some 20,000 years ago – and these mummies can be compared and reveal a period of time when the *Alien Visitor* lived among our ancestors and brought about the leap in intelligence in *Homo sapiens*. This will finally explain the 'missing link' in our evolution and prove that this extra-terrestrial was our ancestor.

Chapter 10

THE ALIEN AND APE WITHIN US

We have our roots in the ground because we evolved as part of the development of life on Earth. But I also think every human is reaching for the stars because another part of our make-up comes from an extra-terrestrial which has left our planet. In the future, gene studies of humans – in connection with research into the genes preserved in mummies and in our nearest ancestors from the ape family – could reveal which genes we share with creatures from Earth and which with the *Alien Visitor*. We do not yet have this genetic proof. However, I believe that we can deduce characteristics we must have inherited from the *Alien Visitor* because we do not see them in our closest ancestors living on Earth today. Obviously, there are a huge number of these characteristics and I allow that further research into the ape family may reveal they have even more in common with us than we think.

We know our appearance is given to us, to some extent, by our parents or earlier generations of our families. The colour of our eyes, size of nose, skin colour, length of legs, size of bones or colour of hair can be traced to our relations. The first comments about a new baby are often about appearance and which physical features belong to which parent or grandparent – diplomacy can be important at this time! For better or worse, families exert their pull across generational lines and over the barriers of time and space. If we have been brought up in a family group, we can find out for ourselves where we have or have not inherited some of our genes.

So far, we have no record of what the *Alien Visitor* looked like but I think it might have had some features which humans have today. I suggest this because there are some aspects of a human appearance that members of the ape family do not share. I believe humans are distinguished from the ape family by the influence of the *Alien Visitor* so by the process of deduction could we say the ways in which we do not look like apes are the ways in which we look like the *Alien Visitor*. The main physical difference between humans and their nearest relative on Earth - the African chimpanzee – is the layer of subcutaneous fat attached to the skin that is unique to man producing his nakedness. So could the *Alien Visitor* also have been naked instead of hairy. Humans are also able to stand upright for most of the time and walk differently from apes which, although they can stand upright, spend much time on their knuckles and consequently have a wrist anatomy quite different from that of humans. Maybe the *Alien Visitor* was also an upright creature. Incidentally, we have early drawing depicting winged creatures which we do not recognise as existing today and winged humans are mentioned in the Dead Sea Scrolls. Even today we frequently depict angels. It might be that the original drawings depict the *Alien Visitor*. If so, we obviously did not inherit these wings but the body of the *Alien Visitor* may have slowly adapted to conditions on Earth varying from those on its own planet. Perhaps the gravity or atmosphere on the aliens' planet allowed them to fly but they could not get off the ground on Earth. Maybe this is why the wings did not survive the continuing evolution of humans after the *Alien Visitor* left. We have always had examples of humans who have physical peculiarities that are not shared by the majority. Circuses have presented so-called 'freaks' to the world. Maybe these people have inherited a feature of the *Alien Visitor* which, like wings, died out because they did not give the developing human an advantage in his survival. However, scientists in the future may be able to find a way of creating people who can fly, perhaps by manipulating thousands of genes that control the development of wings, all synchronised to create the necessary tissue and bones.[22]

We also depict creatures in mythology that were half man half horse (centaur), half woman half fish (mermaid). Did these creatures actually exist as part of the *Alien Visitors'* genetic experimentations on Earth, but failed to evolve? Does the fact that scientists today are manipulating genes from one species to another, for example from jellyfish to mouse, confirm the inheritance of the *Alien Visitor* gene?

Another way in which humans differ from every other animal is in our responses to emotions such as fear. A part of any animals' brain, called the amygdala, detects signs of danger and triggers an instant neuromuscular response. But in humans, another part of the brain which is called the cortex – and is the site of our perception and intelligence – can sometimes control the amygdala. This means that, unlike other animals, the emotions produced in humans are not purely instinctive but coupled with a

---

[22] Michio Kaku *Visions* Oxford University Press 1998

kind of thought process. I think this explains why we experience a far greater and more intricate range of emotions than any other animal. We have this extra capacity in our brain because we inherited it from the *Alien Visitor*. Feelings of love, happiness, fear and anger give humans the ability to know themselves probably better than apes know themselves. Yet emotions are not entirely rational as they seem to occur at random and are not states of mind which can be willed. There is much we do not understand about our emotions but it is difficult to fake them and perhaps this is because we need to be able to rely on them as a kind of universal language when we cannot communicate in any other way.

Linked with this, humans are the only animals to have a complicated approach to experiencing sensations. Other animals feel fear or hunger so that they know when to protect themselves or eat. Obviously, humans have this too. But in addition to this, humans will put themselves through ordeals, such as bungee jumping or self-starvation, in order to bring these sensations upon themselves. Unlike all other animals, as far as we know, humans will have sex to enjoy the sensation, not just to procreate. We know elephants, for example, suffer grief but humans do not just suffer grief, but attempt to understand it and share it. We also try to create other sensations such as that gained from the buzz of a crowd at a pop concert by organising these concerts and making sure lots of people will be there. Humans go to great lengths to bring sensations upon themselves and share them. It seems we must have got this capacity from the *Alien Visitor* because there is no evidence of similar behaviour in any of our ancestors on Earth. It is a by-product of our highly intelligent brains. Perhaps participation in mass hysteria indicates our unconscious desire to express this incomprehensible complexity of emotions with others, spurring each other on to recognise our intelligence from the *Alien Visitor*, unique to our species. The Ancient Greeks seem to have realised this human compulsion to experience sensation and share it with others when the state organised festivals to celebrate the god Dionysus. The idea was to allow citizens to indulge in activities provoking mass hysteria with the hope that they would get it out of their systems in a couple of days and be well-ordered rather than frustrated or wild citizens for the rest of the year.

Another characteristic which I believe we must have inherited from the *Alien Visitor* – because it is not obvious in the ape family – is our ability to comprehend very complicated mathematical ideas such as calculation, logic, astrology, astronomy and measurement. Even people who say they are not good at mathematics are able to work out sums or tell the time – a feat beyond the intelligence of all other animals. We might dismiss mathematics as irrelevant to our lives after we pass the required tests at school but as K.C. Cole explains in *The Universe and the Teacup* we express much of our understanding of the world through mathematics:

Mathematics seems to have an astonishing power to tell us how things work, why things are the way they are and what the universe would tell us if we could only learn to listen. This comes as a surprise from a branch of human activity that is supposed to be abstract, objective and devoid of sentiment.[23]

---

[23] K.C. Cole *The Universe and the Teacup* Little, Brown and Co (UK) 1998

Our democratic voting systems, rational approaches and solutions to often highly emotional questions about fairness, and decisions about how we measure up to other people all involve maths. We put numerical measures onto everything from how fat to how fast, how tall to how small, to how much we should earn and even how much we should love. I think this interest in figures is part of our heritage from the *Alien Visitor*. It seems obvious this visitor must have been obsessed with numbers in order to calculate a space flight and land successfully on Earth. In the earlier chapters I have also described how many of the structures – which I am convinced were built by the *Alien Visitor* – were constructed according to precise mathematical ideas which match our own. For example, it seems possible the mathematical concept *Pi* could have been used in the building of the pyramids in Egypt. Even the composing and performing of music can be seen as an expression of mathematical ability. Although many animals respond to music, we are the only race to have such a large interest in music and ability to produce it that we have devised instruments and methods of composing and performing. Alongside that we have invented many ways of recording and playing music. Everyone has a piece or kind of music they like. It is hard to imagine any human who does not have an opinion on something to do with music. We have evidence that music was performed, dating back thousands of years. Recently, a set of six exquisitely made bone flutes were excavated at a site in China and are believed to be up to 9,000 years old. The composition of music is directly allied with mathematics because it uses time, equations and calculations. We have evidence of talented composers who also excel at maths.

So far, our research into the intelligence of animals has not given us any proof that they have a concept of a long-term future. We do not believe animals are aware they will die until they feel ill or are in danger, whereas we await our deaths all of our lives. I think this also gives humans a more complex attitude to survival. Animals obviously have this as an 'instinct' but humans are able to use this faith in the future to think about survival in more convoluted ways. In his book *Man's Search for Meaning*, [24] Viktor E. Frankl describes his experiences as a prisoner at Auschwitz and other concentration camps during the Second World War. He wrote about how he came to believe survival depended not merely on the daily struggle to stay alive, but on a sense of purpose, which in his incarcerated state meant a belief in the future. He writes:

We must never forget that we may find meaning in life, even when confronted with a hopeless situation. They can take your freedom away. But if suffering is unavoidable and inescapable, they can never take away your inner freedom to face it with courage and dignity.

Frankl survived these appalling wartime experiences to become head of the neurological department of the Polyclinic Hospital in Vienna.

We seem to be the only creatures on the planet which measure and record time. I am in no doubt that we have inherited this from the *Alien Visitor* who must have travelled through space and time to reach Earth. It is likely any craft used to travel from one planet to another would contain instruments used to measure or indicate speed, distance, direction and destination in a similar way

---

[24] Viktor E. Frankl *Man's Search for Meaning* Beacon Press ©1959, 1962, 1984, 1992

to our spacecraft. I think it is possible to say the visitor flew above the planet and was able to have aerial views of it because some unexplained phenomena – such as the Nazca lines – which I believe were created by the *Alien Visitor*, must have been built with an awareness of this perspective. The lines – which I have described earlier in the book – include outlines of animals that can be best appreciated from a height. The Navy has a chart – called the Piri Re'is map - which shows South America, part of Africa and an area of coastline that is buried beneath the Antarctic today. Although this map is dated 1513, there is a chance it could have been copied from an earlier drawing because it seems fantastic such a map could have been made in this period when there were no aircraft. Maybe the original was made by the *Alien Visitor* which – with its craft or unknown powers – could use a higher perspective denied to us until the creation of our own balloons, aircraft and satellites.

I think the measurement of time, along with concepts of speed, direction, distance and destination, did not exist on our planet until the *Alien Visitor* arrived, bringing the knowledge with it. However, I do not think it would be true to say our early *Homo sapiens* ancestors were not aware of the changing seasons and of the ageing of their bodies and of the time it takes for wounds to heal. There are many ways in which time seems to impact on us even though we are not conscious that we are watching time. For example, when we are younger, time seems longer. As we grow older, things seem to pass by quicker. If we are engrossed in an exciting sports event, play, book or a situation that makes us anxious, such as an exam, time seems to pass quickly. Alternatively, we are probably all familiar with the sensation of the terrible delay before an event we are eagerly anticipating. Most people have probably uttered the saying 'a watched kettle never boils'. Even if we did not have clocks we would still have these sensations of things happening rapidly or slowly and I surmise our early ancestor may have had all of this. Even without the regularity of birthdays or important calendar dates it is still possible to sense a person is becoming older and to see weather patterns and the growth and death of types of plants repeating themselves. But it is unlikely our early ancestors – before the arrival of the *Alien Visitor* – would have evolved enough to have formulated theories of time or studied the planets. At this point in their evolution they would probably have been too consumed with understanding the effects of nature on the planets and techniques for survival. Time – or something very similar to our concept of time – was critical for the *Alien Visitor*. It could be argued that the various megaliths and pyramids dotted around the planet were used by the *Alien Visitor* to understand Earth's position in the universe or even to relay this to their own planet.

We are fascinated with time. We measure out all our seconds, seasons and cycle around the sun. We hold competitions where athletes, cars and horses beat each other within thousandths of a second. We also study history, constantly making comparisons between the past and present and even try to relive moments in time on anniversaries of events. We have become obsessed with time and speed. We buy cars based on how fast they can travel despite speed restrictions on every road. We study the speed a tennis ball leaves the racket and use this as one of the ways to measure the talent of tennis players. We set certain times in the day when we will stop to eat –

whether we are hungry or not. Many philosophers and scientists have studied time. Parmenides, the Greek philosopher, proposed in the fifth century BC, that time might be a figment of the imagination. But his theory was largely ignored. What prevailed was the view that things occur one after another. Copernicus, the sixteenth-century astronomer argued the division of time into days and years was not part of a divine master plan but was a product of the Earth's rotation and orbit around the Sun. Isaac Newton said time is a constant, an immutable quality that permeates everything. He argued it is a fundamental component of the universal laws of nature, from which can be calculated what has happened in the past and what will happen in the future. Twentieth-century science has reshaped Newton's view of time but not overthrown it. Einstein observed that time is not constant in its motion. In his theory of relativity, he predicted that time speeds up or down depending on the velocity at which the object travels and the gravity it experiences, that is to say that time runs more slowly for an object that is fast moving. It is an effect that can only be easily observed at speeds close to that of the speed of light but it has been demonstrated in experiments in which aircraft measure time using ultra-sensitive atomic clocks. For example, two of these cesium clocks were synchronised and one went on a round trip from Frankfurt to Boston and back to Frankfurt. The clock on the flight was found to be 0.000,000,0288 seconds slower than the one which remained behind at the Physikalisch-Technische Bundesanstalt (national metrology institute). As we ourselves have started to travel around the world and universe our knowledge of time and its relationship with movement, speed and distance has increased. We have also become aware of new phenomena, such as time zones and the effect travel between them can have on us. With the introduction of faster means of transport and communication, we have seen our lives become progressively 'faster and faster' and more dependent on time. We are speeding up our lives and subsequently our rapid technological development. We have a great interest in travelling at speed that we do not share with any other animals. We get such thrills from travelling at high speed that we have invented fast cars, planes and rollercoasters.

Roller-coaster rides have been in use since the seventeenth century and have become progressively faster and more challenging on the body. Future fairground rides are likely to rocket us skywards from 0-60mph in less than a second and drop us from heights of 180ft – at more than 60mph. Even the development of rollercoasters is thwarted by limitations of the body which is acceleration-limited. If a roller-coaster is built too high in order to go faster, the first curve will produce a g-force greater than can be tolerated. Faster rides would need to be larger and longer to make curves less pronounced to reduce the rotational effect, which should not exceed four times the force of gravity.

In 1997 Andy Green drove ThrustSCC into the record books when he became the first man to set a supersonic land-speed record at just over 763mph. A company in Seattle is designing a small jet-like vehicle which it hopes will take paying passengers 62 miles into space – above the ozone layer where the sky turns black – far enough from Earth's gravitational pull to achieve weightlessness and sensational views of Earth. NASA is already studying the possibility of flying to and eventually colonising Mars – a trip that would cover a distance of over 100 million miles and take two and a half years to complete. It will combine great biological hazards with the stress of being trapped with other people for at least 30 months. These Mars travellers must be willing to sacrifice their health and endure bone decay, muscle wastage and many months of potentially lethal cosmic rays. Scientists will assess candidates, eliminating anyone predisposed to a number of cancers and other medical 'weaknesses'.

I believe that although the extra-terrestrial gene has created within us a desire and ability to travel into space, our bodies are not properly equipped at this stage of our evolution to cope with the stresses and strains of distant space travel.

As geologists plan to declare an end to the Holocene, the era covering the 18,000 years since the last ice age and the start of the Anthropocene – the "age of man", will scientists evolve us on from *Homo sapiens* to ©*Supernus sapiens* (©*Super Sap*)? To head for the stars, we will need to be exceptionally robust - which of course in time will be possible. To get there we will need the latest technologies. I look forward to the future when biology meets silicon.

Since the first man was launched into space, are we entering a new era where we recognise and aim to become an important part of the Universe? The new era brings a huge change in human psychology. We are no longer content in exploring our habitat and just being one of Earth's creatures. Our place in the universe now beckons.

I do not want it to appear as if I am arguing that the qualities we have from the ape are the dark side of our nature and those from the *Alien Visitor* constitute our better part. I think there are qualities or behaviour displayed by humans that we do not see in the animal kingdom. There are obviously several examples but I would like to focus on one. Throughout history we have numerous examples of humans forcing others to live as slaves. When the Spanish conquered a large part of the New World in the late fifteenth century, they put the Indians to work in their mines and fields. The Indians, however, died quickly because of exposure to European diseases and harsh working conditions. To remedy this problem, the Spaniards began importing slaves from Africa in 1517. The Africans were sent first to the West Indies and then to the mainland, where the sugar industry was flourishing. Thus began the harsh institution of black plantation slavery. The first African slaves in North America arrived at the English colony of Virginia aboard a Dutch ship in 1619. The English were then developing highly profitable plantations where tobacco, sugar, and, later, cotton were grown. As the number of slaves required to work in the fields increased, trading in slaves became even more profitable than exporting crops, and an elaborate trade triangle network was set up between North America, the West Indies, and West Africa. In 1681 there were about 2000 slaves in Virginia, but by the mid nineteenth century, the slave population in America had risen to more than 4,000,000. A society's attitude toward its slaves depended on various factors. Generally, the greater the difference between the racial, ethnic, or cultural characteristics of the slave and those of his owner, the worse the slave's condition was and the fewer rights he had. In Rome, for example, where both owners and slaves were white, the slaves were often released. The same thing happened in Africa in cases where both owners and slaves were black but not when they were of different colours. In the American South, however, where the owners were mostly of white European stock and the slaves were of black African stock, the degree of social isolation and the contempt for slaves was extraordinary. For centuries, before Europeans began shipping black people to the Americas in the fifteenth century, Africa had its own flourishing market in slaves. Warring African groups frequently enslaved the captives they acquired in war and the native rulers were only too willing to sell them on to the Portuguese, French, Dutch and English traders who paid them handsomely. Even by the late eighteenth century, when the export of slaves to the Americas was at its height, there were probably more black people in some form of servitude in Africa than there were on the plantations of the New World. What is now Nigeria once abounded with slave markets satisfying indigenous demand. White captives – kidnapped in coastal raids on England, Ireland, France and Italy – were particularly fashionable as eunuchs in the harems of North Africa. In the four centuries after the first Portuguese slaving expedition to West Africa in 1444, some 12 million black people were bought, branded and shipped across the Atlantic to work for plantation owners of the Americas. There are examples of apparently humane and cultivated men who regarded a large proportion of people as slaves. These include Aristotle and St Paul, some Quakers such as William Penn who was a slave-owner and even a number of Popes. Even John Locke – the English philosopher who led the

Enlightenment movement in England and France, inspired the constitution in the United States, and was the author of, among other works, *An Essay Concerning Human Understanding* – held shares in the Royal Africa Company, the leading British exporter of slaves. It might be almost two centuries since William Wilberforce led his great abolitionist campaign, but it is less than 60 years since slavery was practised extensively in Eastern Europe by Nazis, who, like us, listened to Mozart and Beethoven, and were kind to cats. Today, there are still tens of thousands of people in places such as Mauritania and southern Sudan living as slaves to Arab masters. We have a huge number of words in English to describe the structure of slavery, such as 'master', 'slave', 'boss' and 'worker'. We are the only animal on the planet which forces others to work for us. Not only do we have a history littered with examples of slavery but we also use all sorts of animals for work, food, as pets or entertainment. There is evidence that most species of animals live in societies with hierarchies and leaders but none that other animals treat lower orders cruelly or use different species to carry out work. It may be that we are yet to uncover this behaviour in other animals but I surmise the type of power exercised by slave-owners and even lion-tamers is unique to humans and possibly comes from our *Alien Visitor* gene. We can have no idea how the *Alien Visitor* was received on Earth and whether there was instant harmony between the visitor and other creatures or fighting before the visitor bent others to its will. I do believe the visitor was able to exploit Earth's creatures in order to build its civilisations and spread its gene on the planet. This was because the *Alien Visitor* had greater intelligence than any of the other creatures, similar to the position humans hold today. That is to say, although we are terrified of a confrontation with a tiger we have an ability beyond that of the tiger to invent a weapon with which to protect ourselves.

Although it is tempting to argue that many of our baser and more instinctive qualities come from apes I accept there are also examples of good characteristics which we share with apes and would have probably gained whether the *Alien Visitor* had arrived or not. Of course, it is entirely possible that the *Alien Visitor* just happened to have these characteristics too and that it may have – in the many billions of years before its arrival on Earth, evolved from ape-like creatures. We share simple skills such as how to find and eat food and avoid pain which is obviously essential for living. Some more complicated characteristics we share with members of the ape family – although perhaps to different extents – are curiosity and the keenness to learn, the attempts to fit into a society and gain status, the desire for organisation in daily life and the need to spend time with family and friends. We can see evidence of these altruistic instincts in human life where we live, work and play in groups, tribes, clans, teams, clubs, companies and even search for like-minded individuals on the internet!

Examples in nature show that the continuation of a species depends on sharing and is an aspect of everyday life. It is well known that creatures as varied as vampire bats and stickleback fish put their own lives at risk to feed their own young. But we also have examples of some animals helping others such as birds travelling long distances on the backs of elephants. And this favour is reciprocated by the birds which clean their hosts. The economic history of the world teaches us that people, nations and businesses that open up to the world get richer, healthier, wiser and safer than those that try to live behind barriers of protection. Prosperous nations are those that are able to trade with a large number of other nations and share each other's exports. We can get our movies from America, our software from India, our medicines from Switzerland, our financial services from Britain, our mangetouts from Kenya and our philosophy from France, just to give a few examples. The more efficient each is at supplying the other, the more countries can afford to spend on welfare, education and health. All the countries, which have tried to impose regimes that are hostile to those in other parts of the world, have suffered such as China, Russia and America in the 1930s. In recent times Burma and North Korea have tried to isolate themselves. This process of sharing – which we see being carried out by numerous species – plays an important part of our evolution. Perhaps, even without the *Alien Visitor*, we would have become as developed as we are today. It just would have taken a lot longer!

I think we can pinpoint developments in the on-going evolution of humans that are not occurring in the ape family and are perhaps evidence of changes that are being triggered by the *Alien Visitor* gene. Research shows the length of human life is increasing and will continue to do so in the future. Of course, there are social factors affecting this statistic such as better health care for older people and advances in the way illnesses are diagnosed and treated. It could be that we have inherited the ability to live longer from the *Alien Visitor*. Although we have no way of knowing the life span of the visitor we do have many tales of people living extremely long lives, thousands of years ago. There is a list of some of these people in the Bible and Noah is well known for his longevity. In Greek myths there are people who find ways of living for a long time such as The Sybil. The quest for eternal youth has fired the imagination of ageing kings and emperors throughout history. Perhaps these stories were prompted by the length of the *Alien Visitor* life. Or, it could be that it is the intelligence we have gained from the visitor which is enabling us to come up with ways of living for a long time. Researchers believe around 90 per cent of visible signs of ageing are due to ultraviolet light and are trying to conquer the effects of ageing. There are numerous beauty products, containing many different types of chemicals, which aim to stop the ageing process in many different ways. Rapid breakthroughs in DNA research are beginning to tease apart the secrets of the ageing process. Surprisingly, scientists have found that certain cells live indefinitely. Some cells routinely defy the laws of ageing and have no measurable life span. Even some animals have been found to have no fixed life span, such as alligators. Apparently, their cells never lose the ability to reproduce. This may point to the existence of age genes. Scientists have identified an enzyme that helps to protect cells from ageing. Researchers believe cytosolic catalase and a protein called CTL-1 protect cells from oxidative damage which produces ageing in animals, including humans. The search for an age gene – which may retard or repair molecular damage due to ageing – is on. Scientists are also studying whether the body's cells contain genetic information capable of re-generating organs. Sometime in the future we may even eliminate ageing. Incidentally, the idea cannot be discounted that the reason the *Alien Visitor* itself might have enjoyed long life is because it developed techniques of increasing life-span as we are trying to do.

Another example of how the human race, as a whole, is developing in a way that other animals are not is that people are becoming taller. In the last 100 years, the average height of a man in Britain has increased by more than 15 cm (six inches). As with longevity, this may also be triggered by the *Alien Visitor* gene. Although we cannot know the *Alien Visitor* was tall we do have many myths of giants in Greek mythology such as the Titans or Cyclops. Ancient Irish myths name a giant called Finn. Archaeologists have found graves in Egypt that are believed to date back to a time before the time of the pharaohs. They discovered remains in the graves with larger skulls and bodies than those of other remains from that period.[25] I am not suggesting this is conclusive evidence of an *Alien Visitor* but it does confirm the existence of unusually tall people living in this period.

A final example of how I think our evolution is accelerating today in contrast to that of other animals, is communication. Although other animals are able to communicate with each other and have 'languages' they are not able to communicate with their counterparts in all areas of the world, as far as we know. Apart from the explosion in inventions which help us communicate – such as Morse code, telephones and the internet – we are also steadily moving towards a universal language, particularly in business and commerce. English has become more widespread and also an acronymic and logo 'language' is evolving where, for example, a large corporation can be identified anywhere in the world by a

---

[25] W B Emery *Archaic Egypt* Penguin Books 1991

sign or symbol. I believe we may have gained this desire and ability to be able to communicate with anyone, despite distance, from the *Alien Visitor*. There are stories suggesting that at one time, early in our history, we all shared the same language, such as the Tower of Babel story in the Bible. We have also found evidence of languages shared by peoples living miles apart. There are links between the Guanche language - belonging to a race of people from the Canary Islands who were cut off from the rest of mankind until the Spaniards conquered them at the turn of the fifteenth century – and Dravida which is the sacred, pristine language of the Dravidian populations of India. We have only discovered recently that they are remarkably similar in phonetics and in grammar because for many thousands of years we have had no way of knowing many of the languages of people who live very far away from us.

Hopefully, these examples have given an explanation as to why we are so different from other animals on Earth, even our closest ancestors. I hope that by understanding we have this *Alien Visitor* gene we will be able to understand more of ourselves and not just the characteristics which we can see reflected elsewhere in nature. By studying our *Alien Visitor* characteristics we might be better positioned to understand ourselves and answer questions about who we are, where we are going and how we can be better. I believe that if we all know we all have this potential for genius in our genes from the *Alien Visitor* then we are able to make more choices about our lives. Instead of comparing ourselves to apes and congratulating ourselves on what we have already achieved we can compare ourselves to the *Alien Visitor* and inspire ourselves with all the other things we can do.

I think we can feel unhappy, frustrated and trapped because we feel we are not good at something or cannot see anyone in our family and society who offers us any alternatives but I also believe we are making these decisions when we do not realise how much choice we have. As I have said before we all have the potential for genius because that is what makes us human – and separates us from other animals – and if we believe this we can fight for it and aim to lift ourselves up to the greatest heights we can reach. In the future we may learn that just as we have genes engendering criminal behaviour, depression and even bad luck we also have an *Alien Visitor* gene that carries the potential to overcome these other negative genes. We will no longer be able to blame our genes for our natures because we all have the choice and resources to make the most of the positive way of life offered by the *Alien Visitor* gene. Of course, we may also learn our *Alien Visitor* gene has negative qualities we can exploit as well but this will be further choice. I believe we are exceptionally lucky as human beings because, owing to our mixed genes from the *Alien Visitor* and ape, we have two sets of good and bad characteristics and therefore twice as many chances to be the best, or worst, we can be.

Chapter 11

IT'S ALL IN THE MIND

If we can accept this *Alien Visitor* gene theory, I believe we could learn more about ourselves because it is this extra-terrestrial gene that has helped us evolve into the species that we are and sets us so far apart from other animals on Earth. As I have shown earlier, much of the evidence of the *Alien Visitor*'s civilisations seems to have been lost or to have been reinterpreted by subsequent civilisations. It is hard to gain a clear picture of this ancestor. But I think there is another way we can learn about our inheritance and understand our intelligence and that is by focusing on the *Alien Visitor* gene within all of us.

Somehow this gene has given us all a subconscious memory, which comes from the *Alien Visitor*. We have a memory of information that we would not have otherwise learnt on Earth. I think this memory is similar to the Collective Unconscious described by the psychiatrist Carl Jung[26]. He says this Collective Unconscious lies beneath the personal unconscious and is shared by all humanity. He says it is a legacy of a common past, which is stored within us and awaits discovery. Jung said that when treating patients he found they described seeing similar images in their dreams and that these images could also be found in the myths of many cultures. Jung argued that

---

[26] Carl Jung *Psychology of the Unconscious* 1912

people could attach significance to an object or idea without knowing why, only feeling by impulse that it was important. He said this occurred when people became aware of something in their Collective Unconscious.

Jesus referred to this higher state of consciousness as the Kingdom of Heaven; others have named it the Fourth Dimension.

I want to explore how something like this Collective Unconscious or *Alien Visitor* memory is related to our conscious lives. I want to explore this subconscious memory because I think it explains our intelligence, creativity and imagination, which far exceed that of the species which almost share our genetic makeup. Realising that we share a common memory could create a greater understanding between humans of different races, religions, ages and sexes. What we share in common should be more important than the things that divide us. Maybe the growing recognition that we are one of many intelligent life forms in the universe will trivialize the differences between humans?

I am convinced we are born with the *Alien Visitor* gene and that with this gene comes a memory from the *Alien Visitor*. As we are all born with this gene we all have this memory so it can be seen as collective. It is a subconscious memory because it is not made up of experiences we have during our own lifetimes but comes with us at birth. A similar idea can also be found in Plato. Plato believed ideas were implanted in the mind before it became imbedded in the body. According to Plato, birth clouded the mind so the individual forgot all that he knew. Plato thought all knowledge was located in the mind and gained from experiences before birth.

However, Plato believed that through a process of questioning it was possible to cause the mind to remember what it had known before birth. Socrates often referred to a mystical inner voice or 'force' that guided his actions.

One expression of our subconscious memory is our memory of the future. We have an expectation of the future but obviously have no experience with which to have this certainty. Our sense of the 'future' differentiates us from other life-forms. It is important to clarify what I mean by 'future'. All creatures have a memory, the ability to think and predict the future to some extent otherwise they would not survive! Birds know when to migrate and all animals know where and when their food will appear, according to the seasons. However, the desire to have some idea of what will be happening tomorrow, next week, next month or next year is a distinctly human characteristic. A very important aspect of our education and working lives is learning about time and its passage and understanding how to deal with and organise time. We are taught to think ahead and plan for tomorrow and much of our success in life can depend upon forward planning. We also use the experiences we have already gained to make predictions about our future and to alter it. We know that if we are unhappy with a present situation we can make it different for the future. The future can promise greater security but humans always know that it will also include death. With the advent of the nuclear bomb and awareness of the depleting ozone layer, we have also become concerned not only about our own future but the future of the planet, the human race and even the universe.

People can use their knowledge and experience – gained through their lives – to predict events involving family members or colleagues at work because they have observed patterns. We predict what will happen by extrapolating information or statistics from data that we have already gathered as for example in general elections or weather forecasts or the outcome of football matches. These kinds of predictions are empirical because they are based on data that has been collected through experience, observation and perhaps measurements. If we have gained any kind of specialist knowledge – which our friends and colleagues do not share – we might be considered prophetic. For example, I have been privileged to work, and in my small way influence, the direction of many rapidly evolving industries in the realm of computer and semiconductor technology. In the 1970s, I was able to 'predict' to friends and dinner guests a view of the future using my specialist knowledge. My friends listened with amazement as I talked of 'hole-in-the-wall' cash dispensers, a cashless society with the introduction of 'smart cards', shopping via a combined computer and TV in the home, e-mail and video e-mail. However, I think we have a capacity to believe in and sometimes predict the future in a non-empirical way. Even if we do not actually make successful predictions, we still feel that we may be able to. We may be sceptical about our powers to do this but the fact is that generation after generation has believed in individuals with various powers of prediction or intuition, such as fortune-tellers, seers and clairvoyants. We enjoy watching sci-fi films where writers predict the future of our planet. For thousands of years we have put faith in non-empirical methods of telling the future, such as horoscopes, chiromancy (palmistry), Tarot (fortune-telling) cards, and studying crystal balls. Horoscopes or astrology are so popular that almost every popular newspaper and magazine contains a regular column. Most people know their star sign. We are interested in prophecies that are not based on empirical knowledge such as prophecies of impending natural disasters. I do not believe these prophecies are transmitted into our minds when we are asleep or meditating. Rather, I think the information is already there from the day we are born yet most of us are unaware of it for most of our lives. Prophecy seems to happen spontaneously but is this because prophets have somehow managed to tap into their subconscious minds, voluntarily or involuntarily, unlocking the information already within their memories? I do not think these prophecies are received but are recovered. Monks, magicians, mediums and mediators all invoke prophetic powers by sitting in a relaxed state and opening themselves up as a channel for what will or will not pass through them.

Sacred music, drumming, repetitious mantras, incense, hallucinogenic drugs or chemicals, sympathetic places, symbolic imaginary or a host of other aids or devices may inspire the transmissions. The famous American clairvoyant Edgar Cayce (1877-1945) was able to enter a trance on demand simply by lying down in his office. Although we are interested in accessing our hidden memory I do not think we have many, if any, proven examples of someone doing this so successfully that they have managed to read a prophecy and decipher it. Prophets are often unaware of the implications of their transmission. Prophetic pronouncements are much like dreams in that they are often difficult to order in time, or to decipher. Some of the most important prophets were unable to interpret their own prophecies. Probably, the most famous prophet is Nostradamus[27]. He was born in 1503 in Provence, France. He published his prophecies in a book *Prophéties*. Nostradamus claimed he had visions which he converted into four-line quatrains which make up *Prophéties*. He has been credited by many with predicting the Great Fire of London, the French and Russian Revolutions, Napoleon, Hitler, the assassination of President Kennedy and the Gulf War. Although Nostradamus is the most famous clairvoyant in Western culture, there is not one single example in the whole of the Nostradamian literature where a commentator has accurately unscrambled the meaning of a predictive verse prior to the event it predicted. We can be cynical about Nostradamus and a logical part of our minds may revolt against the idea that he predicted future events but there is a part of the human psyche which, generally, is attracted to the idea of Nostradamus' predictions. For example, when earthquakes rocked Italy in 1997, bookshops sold out of his works. Nostradamus' prophecies appeal to many people. Evidence of this is his fame today – nearly five hundred years after he made his predictions. *Prophéties* or versions of his predictions are still available in most bookshops around the world. Perhaps our fascination with Nostradamus comes from the fact that his predictions are vaguely familiar to us and are part of the memory we have from the *Alien Visitor*. It would be wrong to abstract Nostradamus and his visions from the society in which he lived. He was not a hermit who produced his predictions for his own interests. He was patronised by aristocracy and I think it would be naïve to ignore the fact his work was produced in a very political

---

[27] David Ovason *The Secrets of Nostradamus* Century Books 1997

context where it was important for Nostradamus to remain in favour with his patrons. We must recognise that Nostradamus had a talent which he realised was marketable. In the sixteenth century, predictions were lucrative. It was commonplace for the horoscopes of the famous individuals to be published – sometimes even against their will. Many people read horoscopes or constructed charts and read what would happen from them. The moves of significant people were scrutinised and predicted according to horoscopes. All this might explain why the quatrains in *Prophéties* are in such an obscure form. Nostradamus might be seen to have walked a fine line between wanting to appear as if he had important prophecies to pass on which would be of value to his patrons and not wanting to be classed as a heretic. He had to remain popular. If his quatrains had many meanings he could offer alternative translations to those insisting he may have said something controversial. Nostradamus may well have also realised that knowledge is power and by creating versatile language he could control his prophecies and guarantee his position, as no one else would be able to decipher his words without his help. Over the centuries, scholars of Nostradamus have wrestled with the various languages in the quatrains – a kind of French dialect, scattered with Latin, Greek and Italian and containing esoteric references. Because *Prophéties* is not clearly written, we have to be very careful that we do not manipulate and interpret a prophecy to predict an event. Before the millennium there were fears that the world was coming to an end. One interpretation of a quatrain by Nostradamus is that the end of the world would occur in the seventh month of 1999. A reference to an eagle led some to believe that his apocalypse would fall on America's Independence Day. This determination to get to the bottom of what Nostradamus was saying shows an enduring faith in prophecy so that it is in some ways irrelevant whether Nostradamus was genuine or not. What is important is that there is something in the people living during Nostradamus' lifetime and in subsequent generations that believes in prophecy. If, however, Nostradamus' predictions really were the product of his ability to access his *Alien Visitor* memory gene then it must be asked what made it possible for him to do this when most humans are unable to. Perhaps, awareness of this memory was greater in Nostradamus' time because his generation was closer to the arrival of the *Alien Visitor* than present generations. Or maybe Nostradamus had access to books and other sources which most of his generation were unaware of so that he could collect some of the best popular horoscopes of the time to help produce his *Prophéties*. Nostradamus claimed to be descended from one of ten lost tribes of Israel, the Issachari, who were noted for their prophetic gifts. Nostradamus' grandfather was reputed to be a fine astrologer and perhaps, as discussed in the previous chapter, this gave the young Nostradamus the chance to develop his abilities. Perhaps he was able to use his extensive knowledge of astronomy and astrology – combined with aspects of human psychology which he observed – to interpret his visions. Maybe it is because he possessed all these skills together that he was able to decipher his subconscious memory just as Plato advocated questioning the self to find out what it knew before it was born.

In all of this I am suggesting that the *Alien Visitor* memory contains our future which implies the *Alien*

Visitor knew the future of what would happen on Earth. I want to explain how it could be that the *Alien Visitor* knew our future. The *Alien Visitor* was highly intelligent and even when it arrived on Earth thousands of years ago it had intelligence beyond ours today. But I hypothesise that just as we gained our intelligence from this *Alien Visitor*, so the *Alien Visitor* gained its intelligence in the same way on its own planet from another highly evolved race. This could go back for billions of years throughout the galaxy. Therefore, our memory and intelligence – which we received from the *Alien Visitor* – is the product of billions of years of evolution on a universal scale. We have been the fortunate recipients of the *Alien Visitor* gene, which has dramatically speeded up our evolutionary progress. In our minds, everything we imagine or have yet to imagine has already happened in our *Alien Visitor* history. In other words, we are mimicking the evolution of the *Alien Visitor*. The *Alien Visitor's* history is our future. There is a big difference because we are evolving on Earth and the *Alien Visitor* evolved on a different planet so this may force us to evolve in a slightly different way from the *Alien Visitor*. However, in order for the *Alien Visitor* to have been able to arrive at and live on Earth, our planet must have some vital things in common with their planet. It may be that the *Alien Visitor* came to Earth with the intention of continuing its own history and culture through breeding with the pre-human Ape. The *Alien Visitor* may have realised that with the information – which would eventually be genetically stored in each and every human brain to a greater or lesser degree depending on progeny – we would eventually arrive at their level of understanding and take off into space ourselves to spread this gene even further around the universe.

If a child inherits the *Alien Visitor* gene from its parents then it follows that it will also inherit other non-*Alien Visitor* genes from its parents. The life experiences of parents are transferred onto their children. Freud said that some of the most important things that influence our behaviour and our character are feelings and experiences of which we are not aware. Everyone knows what a 'Freudian slip' is – the sudden, accidental betrayal of a person's true thoughts, unthinkingly blurted out from the subconscious. I have argued that we have a common gene from the *Alien Visitor* and that we share genes with our families. But we are not all the same and we do not lead identical lives. I would like to explore these complex ideas about our memories and consciousness and how they interact. I think I can explain my ideas by likening the human to a computer system.

We can liken the human brain to the computer's central processing unit (CPU) or microprocessor. The nervous system can be compared to the computer's motherboard, which connects all the computer's functions. The human memory can be seen as the computer's memory. Our skin and bones can be likened to the computer's case or chassis and our heart to the machine's power supply. Our sight might be compared with the computer monitor or visual display unit, our ability to create sound with the computer's speakers and our language with the computer's language of binary codes. The internal workings of our bodies could be compared to the In-Band in a computer network and our senses to the Out-Band in a network. Another similarity is that humans and computers are both susceptible to viruses! How could anyone compare the brain to a computer? The brain is a very sophisticated information processor. The neurons in the brain, which give rise to a release of chemicals, are like the electrons in the computer, which compel the machine to release energy to work. Neurons, like electrons, have two functions – they can either trigger or not trigger chemicals, that is to say they are either on or off. A computer's electrons also work in this binary code. The cerebellum in the brain which acts as an autopilot – co-ordinating senses with movement without our being conscious of doing so – can be compared with the microprocessor which co-ordinates the computer. Of course our brains are a lot more advanced than the computers CPU and we differ from artificial systems in that our brains make extensive use of chemicals that enable one neuron to communicate with another. These chemicals can vary in amount and type. In this way, the brain has another dimension of flexibility not yet invented in computers and this explains why we have emotions when computers do not. Nobody has built a computer that feels pain, gets depressed or giggles. The computer always gives logic-based responses. It is not irrational, although at times it may seem so to the frustrated computer user.

When we are born we are similar to a brand-new computer. We have 'hardware', as described above, but we also have 'software' including an 'operating system' - which has already been built into us and gives us our personality and individuality.

It is important to explain the term 'operating system' as used in computers. 'Operating systems' provide a software platform on top of which other programs, called 'application programs', can run. The 'application programs' must be written to run on top of a particular 'operating system'. Your choice of 'operating system', therefore, determines to a great extent the applications you can run. For example you can only run the 'application program' *Word*, *Excel* or a *PowerPoint* presentation from the *Microsoft Office Suite* on one of the most popular 'operating systems' – *Microsoft MSDOS, Windows 95/98/2000, Windows NT®, Windows ME®, Windows XP®, Windows Vista®, Windows 7, Windows 8*... All of these programs reside in Read-Only Memory (ROM). This type of non-volatile memory has been permanently loaded with programs by the manufacturer and cannot be changed.

The 'operating system' is the most important program that runs on a computer. Every general-purpose computer <u>must</u> have an 'operating system' to run other programs. 'Operating systems' perform basic tasks, such as recognising 'input' from the 'keyboard', sending 'output' to the 'display screen', keeping track of 'files' and 'directories' on the 'disk' and controlling 'peripheral devices' such as 'disk drives' and 'printers'.

For large systems, the 'operating system' has even greater responsibilities and powers. It is like a traffic cop – it makes sure those different programs and 'users' running at the same time do not interfere with each other. The 'operating system' is also responsible for 'security', ensuring that unauthorised users do not 'access' the system.

I believe this 'operating system' in humans is comprised of genes from not only our parents but ancestors reaching back to the beginning of life. Within our 'operating systems' I believe we have what I would call a 'transgenerational' subconscious memory which is made up of data gathered from the point when life began to when our life began.

The Catholic Church maintains that the newly fertilised human egg is a "human individual, body and soul", possessing the dignity of the person, who is not just something, but someone". They also argue with the scientific minimalist description of the human egg. An egg is large: 250 times larger than a red blood cell and weighing a hundredfold more and far more complex than the scientific community is willing to concede. This idea of instant divine "ensoulment" at conception is recognised throughout Christianity.

I am inclined to agree with the Catholic Church's view but also wonder if the activity triggered in the human egg at the instant of fertilization is far more astonishing than we could possibly imagine.

If, as I believe we inherit a transgenerational memory, a memory going all the way back to when life began on our planet, then is it possible that all human eggs contain all information of our evolution on Earth, and if our development has been influenced by an alien intervention, then this knowledge could be inter-planetary! Maybe the human egg contains billions of miniscule "creation" cells and is primed with all the instructions to start the miraculous construction of larger human cells, organs, limbs and of course the brain, to produce a remarkably complex individual human being.

In a similar way to a computer, to bring the human egg to life requires energy which is provided at the point of conception by the male sperm together with its contribution of cells/genes.

From the moment life begins, the embryo embarks on a massive de-selection/re-selection process and begins discarding information which is irrelevant to the development of the human being in the womb. This area of understanding the mechanisms for switching genes on and off is being studied by biologists' working in the emerging science of epigenetics. Epigenetics, which is an emerging branch of microbiology, may show the way to 'hack' into our hidden memory. At the heart of this new field of science is a simple idea – that genes have a 'memory'. The BBC Horizon documentary [28]*The Ghost in Your Genes* provided compelling evidence that a memory of an event could be passed through generations.

Could it be that when we are born only a very small fraction of our epigenetic memory gene codes are switched on thus endowing us with our individual genomic imprint? The rest are seen as surplus to requirements and thus switched off. Throughout our lives environmental conditions can affect these switches and turn some of our memory gene codes back on – with astonishing results.

Will exploring epigenetics, via the expanding Epigenome Network, over time, provide the science to enable us to 'switch on' our hidden memory codes and re-trace our detailed and factual history and confirm the existence of an *Alien Visitor* in our not too distant past?

In addition to this we accumulate experiences and information during our life span on Earth that adds to this knowledge and might be likened to an 'application program' similar to *Word* or *Excel*, where we add our

---

[28] *'The Ghost in Your Genes'* screened on BBC Television in November 2005 with contributions from Professor Marcus Pembrey, Professor Wolf Reik, Jonathan Seckl and Lars Olov Bygren

own files in a similar way to adding software and files to a computer's hard disk which gives each computer its individuality. There are some experiences and information which change our personalities and seemed ingrained into us and there are also things which leave little impression on us and this might be compared to a game run on the computer's CD ROM for a few weeks and then never played again. I hope this comparison starts to show how we can be individual even though we are born with common genes. So, it is possible to influence your life span on Earth, but you cannot change your inherited 'operating system'!

Each of us comes this way only once and each of us is uniquely precious by nature from start to finish. I hope the complexity of our multi-million year old 'operating system' demonstrates just how amazing we all are!

During every second of each day, every day of the year, we are constantly moving between these different levels of consciousness. Our thoughts may be a combination of these different kinds of consciousness. We have experiences which cause differences from one person to another. In line with my computer analogy, it could be said we take on different software and do different things with it. This becomes very clear as we progress through our working lives. The memories that we gain from our non-*Alien Visitor* ancestors and during our own lives may alter our *Alien Visitor* memory or make it easier or harder to interpret these embedded ideas. In a computer, a great deal of data gets lost or hidden in the system. Files can be removed, but unless the information on the hard or floppy disk is not completely erased, then some data may remain. This is so common that there is even a term for attempts to resurrect this information. 'Dumpster diving' is the process of trawling through a company's computer system, trying to turn up discarded computer records containing an organisation's financial records, details of research or even employees' pay scales. I had not fully appreciated this problem with secure erasure of data until I witnessed two security men from the Ministry of Defence, dressed in clean-room attire, attend a hard disk drive repair operation. When the computer's platters, which store information, had been removed from the hard disk drive they were immediately given to these MoD men who told me these platters would be taken to an MoD establishment where the disks would be ground into powder. I had also heard cases of industrial espionage, where EPROM (Electrically Programmed Read Only Memory) memory chips were studied under powerful microscopes to detect disturbances in their transistor and electron structures. By interpreting the pattern of these disturbances it is then possible to work out what binary data has been stored in the memory chips. Companies are so concerned about this problem of discarded information remaining on their systems that they spend a lot of money on erasure software packages before they swap or discard their old machines. These packages erase the data in the computer file and also any faint traces that it may have left elsewhere on the storage media.

Just as residues of information can be left in a computer memory, so they can be left in a human memory. If we hear music that we have not heard for a long time it can almost transport us back to that earlier time when we first heard it. The smell of a perfume or even a room can also act in this way, jogging us back to a time which we associate with that smell. But this unearthing of our memories is not only the product of our senses. External situations can also evoke the past. We can recall a repeated television programme that we first saw many years before or recognise the face of friend in a crowd, even though we may not have seen that friend for many years. Chance meetings and Christmas and other festivals can spark childhood memories. If we are reminded of a major news story such as the death of Kennedy, Diana or John Lennon we can often recall exactly where we were and what we were doing when we first heard this news and this memory can be conjured up all through our lives. Re-visiting places that were important to us earlier in our lives can also produce a flood of memories. For example, if we stand outside a childhood home, decades seem to fall away. Even though the house has a new door or the stripling tree you planted is now 15 feet tall, it is still possible to see what used to be there. It is as if we can see two things at the same time, the present and the past. The present-day state of the house is right before your eyes but is taken over by a memory. The same thing can happen with people from the past. When we see a former friend or acquaintance we might even start to feel the way we did when first knew them and remember a string of events and ideas from that time that we otherwise no longer really think about. Things can spring into our minds that we thought we had completely forgotten about or did not believe were significant at the time we first learnt them. In these ways, we involuntarily bring forward memories from our past experiences with a lot of clarity. People who believe they are reincarnations of our ancestors may also be bringing forward memories from our collective memory. I believe these memories are not resurrected from the individual's own life on Earth but from a database of human history which we all possess in our inherited 'transgenerational' memory genes. In extreme cases, some individuals may find it difficult to lead their lives on Earth because of easy access to information stored in the brain of earlier ancestors. So, when Arthur Pendragon claims he is the twentieth-century reincarnation of King Arthur he is perhaps experiencing flashes of information from this 'Transgenerational' subconscious memory, which he has inherited and cannot control. Some people may believe they are reincarnations and others do not, depending on whether or not they have flashbacks from the 'Transgenerational' memory. A computer can also be seen to have 'flashbacks'. We may do a search to find a file and come up with a completely different one that was thought to have been erased several years ago.

Sometimes we experience irrational fears, such as sense of horror when we see spiders, but we have no past experience in our own lives that could explain why we would be so frightened of this creature. This fear is not learnt, it seems to already be within us and is sometimes triggered but we do not know why. Perhaps our phobias and superstitions were once logical to us but during our evolution we have become unclear about why we have these impulses. The knowledge to understand them is still within our subconscious memories but is obscured or has been altered by the addition of more information through the generations. People sometimes suffer so badly from these irrational fears that they try to overcome them using hypnotherapy. Maybe this works because the hypnotherapist is able to draw out the forgotten knowledge in the patient and match it to the trigger so that it is no longer irrational and therefore alarming.

I accept that Yoga, like hypnotherapy, may be used to explore the subconscious or hidden memories which I believe come from the *Alien Visitor* gene which also contains a database of our human history. Yoga induces a state of calm, encouraging information, which may be suppressed by other ways of thinking, to come out. In this way, Yoga might be seen as a kind of 'search engine' allowing the subject to look through the memory – which in this analogy we can compare to the internet – for hidden information. But more than this, I believe this ancient form of meditation was an *Alien Visitor* art. I think the *Alien Visitor* learnt to use a kind of Yoga itself to access its own hidden memories which it would have gained from its ancestors. In turn, the *Alien Visitor* has passed this skill onto us so that we can, ironically, find out more about our *Alien Visitor* memory. As a 'search engine' uses electricity to scan the internet, I think Yoga uses energy from the universe, such as that found in ley lines, to uncover information.

Apart from having memories, we are also contained in the memories of other people. We may meet someone and be reminded of past experiences and sensations, but in the same way other people will meet us and recollect memories associated with us. Even if we do not have children our ideas are still transferred to consequent generations of people because of the impact we make on our peers and even on pets in our own lifetimes. I remember as a child, watching funeral corteges pass by. It so happened that I lived on the route to the cemetery. This was in the north east of Scotland where the culture was for the men to walk behind the hearse. I remember that at some funerals there were barely a handful of men while at others there were processions of hundreds of people from the small community, paying their last respects. They all had recollections of the deceased. The ideas of this now dead person had impinged on some way on all the people at the funeral. They in turn were likely to talk about the dead person, passing the ideas on further and perhaps through generations if there was something about that person which had struck someone as remarkable. Our interest in celebrities, alive and dead, produces a large circulation of information about that person. Newspapers and websites convey these people's ideas to millions of people, sometimes all over the world. There are going to be generations and generations of people in Britain who know something about Princess Diana, probably even hundreds of years after her death.

I think our actions can also enter the consciousness of other people. For example, the Scottish accent, kilt and bagpipes have appeal for many living in French, Dutch, Italian and even German towns and villages. I believe this may have been transferred by the children of those who met the young Scottish soldiers during the First and Second World Wars. We all recognise that a cat loves fish, catches mice and spends a great deal of time on personal hygiene – cleaning itself from top to tail. This behaviour is triggered by genes that have remained unchanged over the centuries that distinguish it as a cat. But over time, the cat's memory may be bombarded with the actions of a human if it is a pet. This can result in a very tame and domesticated cat that prefers chocolate to fish. This is evident with all animals that have become closely associated with humans. Samuel Taylor Coleridge observed "that ants, bees and dogs were gradually evolving moral perceptions." Australians are now allowed to keep dingoes as pets without a special licence, despite the wild dogs' reputation as child-snatchers and cattle-killers. Even those animals which are not kept as pets by humans can be seen to respond to and even evolve according to human actions. For example, pest control specialists have to introduce more exotic flavours to their bait to catch mice used to spicy leftovers. Some mice have also learnt to steer clear of traditional cereal bait. These animals are changing their tastes in response to what we do. Perhaps these examples of how our intelligence can start to affect the intelligence and habits of animals explain how we gained the *Alien Visitor* gene. I suppose our early ancestors may have got this gene and memory not only from breeding with the *Alien Visitor* but also from working with it and being deeply influenced by it.

If our memories can overlap in our own minds and we are a part of other people's memories then is it possible we can share some kind of telepathy? We have all experienced *déjà vu* where we suddenly feel that what felt like a new experience has already happened to us before. At the same time we know this cannot be rational because we know it is impossible that we would have already had that experience. A possible explanation for a *déjà vu* experience is that there is a 'hiccup' in the brain's assimilation process so it presents the same information twice in a very small fraction of a second. Neuroscientists believe that this is caused by a shift in our gaze. For example, a clock can sometimes seem to have stopped for an instant if we suddenly look up to study its ticking second hand. It sometimes appears as if the second hand takes a good deal longer than normal to move on to the next second. The brain can stretch time to suit itself so that our perception of time is quite flexible and might not correspond to physical reality. Neuroscientists believe that the sensation is related to how the brain switches off our vision during the time we shift our gaze. The same effect has been noted when using a telephone. When you call someone, you hear the ringing tone, but the phone is not answered. You go to put the receiver down but at the last moment you decide to check if the person has picked up at the other end. You lift the receiver back to your ear and you get the impression that the ringing tone has actually stopped and you expect to hear someone on the other end. Then the ringing starts again. Just for a moment it seemed as if time had stopped the phone ringing. In this case, movement of the arm, rather than the eyes, can cause the brain to adjust the time at which we perceive the ringing tone – from the moment we moved the receiver, rather than when it arrived at the ear. Alternatively, there are theories that the human body clock is made up of a multiplicity of clocks distributed throughout the body, keeping a daily cycle going in their own domains. This might explain how parts of our bodies respond to incoming information quicker than others, giving us the impression we have already seen something. However, I do not feel these theories on *déjà vu* go far enough because they do not explain the following personal experience I had in 1984. My family were waiting for me at Heathrow Airport on my return from a business trip to Phoenix, Arizona. My youngest daughter, who was nine years old at the time, said to my wife while they were waiting 'Daddy has a bump on his head'. I had not previously mentioned to my wife that I had bumped my head a few days earlier. When I arrived to be greeted by my family, I appeared with a large bump on my head.

How could it be that my daughter could have already seen this bump when she was thousands of miles from where I had been when I had the accident? How can the theories about *déjà vu* explain the long-time delay between my daughter telling my wife about the bump and me appearing before them with the bump? I believe that because we share this *Alien Visitor* gene we are all connected to each other, in the way that a large number of computers can be networked. Perhaps it was due to this shared gene and its interaction with other genes, which I obviously share with my daughter that she had this flash of what I would look like. I think what we call telepathy may well be instances of our 'software' interfacing with the 'software' of other people. A kind of telepathy can be built up between people who know each other well. A friend can call us moments after we have been thinking or talking about them and it is quite common for a couple, siblings or best friends to say the same words at the same time, seemingly quite by chance. Telepathy is a kind of intuition where we feel we know something yet this is not based on any experiences we have had or any empirical knowledge.

When we experience *déjà vu*, our minds seem to recall memories based on our experiences. This tricks us into believing there is a displacement of time in our present conscious lives. But I also believe that as a race, we are trying to decipher memories of events that we have not experienced. I think we can accidentally introduce our past subconscious information, that is to say, data from our ancestors that is stored in our memory to our present conscious memory?

As far as I know, there is no evidence of anyone touching a ghost but many people have 'seen' ghosts. I believe the memory of the ancestor exists in an individual's subconscious memory and under certain conditions the 'video clip' of the ancestor or location can be accessed from the subconscious memory and appears as a 'ghost'. The same process applies to most Unidentified Flying Objects sightings. Many people around the world have 'witnessed' this phenomenon. The subject of UFOs has become so popular that it can now be studied as Ufology. Some claim UFOs are currently mapping our planet. I think they were doing this, 13,000 years ago and where people believe they see UFOs today they are actually seeing an inherited memory hidden in their subconscious.

Our human tissue, our flesh and blood is comprised of a multitude of chemicals. So our brain/memory tissue is by no means a secure means of storing and retaining data. We can observe this as we grow older. The 'links' between the memory cells become weaker and we begin to look back on the memory that is easiest to access, our early memory of our life-span on Earth, our childhood and those we grew up with. As we grow ever older we can become very confused as we slip back into information stored in our memory inherited from previous generations. Much of this uttered information does not make sense to even the closest member of the family. Perhaps, in trying to understand inherited memories we will gain a greater understanding of senility.

We can experience these inherited memories without too much consternation in dreams, nightmares and *déjà vu* experiences, but in extreme cases they can cause mental illnesses such as paranoia and schizophrenia.

The silicon chip is a much more stable method of storing information. However, compared to the human brain, this silicon chip technology and the level of complexity is still in its infancy and computer 'hackers' can gain access to the information stored in these silicon circuits. As mentioned previously all sorts of ways and means have been tried to dislodge or in some way manipulate our memory genes, but we are still some way off before we can 'hack' into the hidden memory in the human brain. I think we can try to excavate this knowledge using our imagination in addition to our intelligence.

Chapter 12

IMAGINATION

Imagination helps us unlock our memories and explore our *Alien Visitor* gene. It is this function which allows us to consider the future. The ability to imagine, to think creatively, is theoretically infinite and may itself be handed down to us by the *Alien Visitor,* as it does not seem that our other ancestors in the animal world possess this faculty. By looking at some of the work of the foremost science fiction writers we can see what they have imagined and perhaps get an idea of the reality of the future.

In some ways, NASA's trips to the moon might be seen to have been possible because of the cultural climate in which the scientists and astronauts grew up. The idea of a moon landing was in the public consciousness at this time thanks to a long list of science fiction stories including Jules Verne's *From the Earth to the Moon* (1865) and Arthur C. Clarke's *A Fall of Moondust* (1961). A generation of young scientists who grew up with time-travel stories like H.G. Wells's *The Time Machine* (1895) and Robert Silverberg's *Up the Line* (1969) were more likely to think about closed time-like curves – such as the celebrated 'wormhole' that creates a short cut in space and time. So in this way the imagination can be seen to have unlocked our *Alien Visitor* knowledge enabling us to travel through space. Wells acquired a reputation within his own lifetime as a prophet. In *The War in the Air* (1908), he foresaw certain developments in the military use of aircraft. In *The First Men in the Moon* and *The War of the Worlds*, he introduced the idea of the Martian which has passed into popular mythology. It will be of no surprise to find that NASA's focus group for long-range planning includes prominent science-fiction authors. In the UK, the Ministry of Defence had a regular weekly order for the comic *The Eagle* for more than a decade, which featured the exploits of Dan Dare, the pipe-smoking pioneer of outer space, his sidekick Digby and that personification of green evil, the Mekon. Some undergraduates taking university courses in science can study the links between their subject and science fiction.

One of the best examples of an imagination that has predicted advances in technology is that of Sir Arthur C. Clarke. From 1941 to 1946 Clarke served in the Royal Air Force, becoming a radar instructor and technician. While in the service he published his first science-fiction stories and in 1945 wrote for *Wireless World* an article entitled 'Extra-Terrestrial Relays', predicting in detail a communications satellite system that would relay radio and television signals all over the world. The reaction of even specialised readers was sceptical. Twenty years later, however, the Early Bird synchronous satellites were actually launched. In the 1960s, Clarke collaborated with motion-picture director Stanley Kubrick in making the innovative and highly praised science-fiction film *2001: A Space Odyssey* (1968). When Clarke and Kubrick created the film, over 30 years ago, they depicted a highly advanced computer called HAL. They tried to make the HAL 9000 as advanced as they could imagine a computer could possibly be in the year 2001, while still remaining plausible.

With the breath-taking developments in microprocessor and communication technology today, we can see the advances taking us to HAL sometime in the future. Indeed, HAL acts much more like a human being trapped within a silicon box than like one of today's high-end Pentium or Athlon workstation or server computer system running the latest Windows, DOS, Linux, Solaris, or Novell Netware 'operating systems'. Throughout the film, HAL talks like a person, thinks like a person, plans – badly, it turns out – like a person, and, when he is about to die, begs like a person. It is HAL's ability to learn and his control of the ship's systems, rather than his ability to perform lightning-fast calculations, that make him such a formidable challenge for the humans when they try to disconnect him. Is this 1960s vision of the future of machine intelligence still realistic today? Yes, although not on the timetable set forth in either the film or Clarke's novel[29].

We can do some things as well as HAL. There is a chess program, Deep Blue, that beats all but a dozen people in the world, and it is improving every year. Likewise, we can build big computers. Building a supercomputer network with the power necessary for performing HAL's functions is just a matter of time.

Today, computers commonly do some of the tasks HAL performs in the movie. HAL guides Discovery to Jupiter. Almost 20 years ago, the United States launched two unmanned Voyager spacecraft, which were largely

---

[29] Sir Arthur C Clarke *2001: A Space Odyssey* Legend 1990

guided by onboard computers, to Jupiter, Saturn, Neptune, Uranus, and beyond.

Likewise, the past 20 years of research and development of Artificial Intelligence have had tangible benefits. AT&T, for example, has been phasing in a speech-recognition system that can understand the words 'collect,' 'calling card,' 'third-number,' 'operator,' 'yes,' and 'no'. That does not seem like a hard job – for a person. Try writing the program and you will soon be coping with hundreds of kinds of accents, high levels of background noise and different kinds of distortion introduced by different kinds of phone lines and telephone instruments. Building a system that can recognise just those six words has taken AT&T more than 40 years of research.

Of course, there is still a big jump in intellect between the AT&T machine that can recognise six words and HAL. And we are still a long way off from getting a machine to truly think and learn. That is a problem that has been haunting the Artificial Intelligence (AI) field for more than 50 years.

How close are today's computers to realising the promise of HAL? When will we be able to talk to a HAL-like computer and consider it nearly an equal? When will the dream of *2001* become reality? Perhaps the easiest way to answer that question is to take a step-by-step look at what it means to be HAL.

HAL is a chatterbox. Unlike today's computers, the primary way HAL communicates with Discovery's crew is through the spoken word. Bowman and Poole speak; HAL listens and understands. How far are we from a computer that can comprehend its master's voice?

Voice recognition is a hard but largely solved problem. Many companies are now selling programs that let you command a personal computer using your voice. These programs get better every time PCs get faster. Today they can recognise more than 60,000 words and control a wide variety of PC applications, including word processors and spreadsheets. Increasingly, they are finding a market among people who simply have not learned to type or have not learned to spell.

Unlike HAL, which could listen to people speaking in a continuous flow, today's systems require that you pause between each word. The programs use the pauses to find where each word begins and ends. The computer then looks up the word in a phonetic dictionary, creating a list of possible matches. An elementary knowledge of grammar helps these programs pick the right word and resolve the difference between homonyms like 'write' and 'right'.

Continuous speech systems use the same kinds of algorithms as today's word-by-word systems but have the added burden of figuring out where each word starts and stops. Making those decisions requires substantially more computing power. However, various companies claim that they have systems that do not require the speaker to pause between words and in effect are close to reaching HAL's level of speech recognition, and progress is picking up. By 2001, we should have it.

Microsoft predict adding 'senses' to the computer including weight and smell and we will soon be able to talk to someone in China for example, in English and this will be translated into Chinese and include all the original intonation of our voice.

HAL can do more than understand spoken words – the computer can also read lips. In one of the film's pivotal scenes, Bowman and Poole retreat to one of Discovery's sealed pods to have a private conversation. HAL watches their lips through the window and realises that the two humans may attempt to disconnect his brain.

Is computerised lip-reading possible? Thirty years later, the debate over the efficacy of pure lip-reading – even in humans – still is largely undecided.

Wade Robison, a professor of philosophy at the Rochester Institute of Technology, where 1,000 of the school's 9,000 undergraduates are profoundly deaf, is sure that lip-reading is possible because human intelligence can master it. Robison remembers one student in particular. He did not have a clue she was deaf until one day he happened to be talking one-on-one with her in his office. He finished up a sentence as he turned to answer the phone, and she had to ask him to repeat the sentence. She needed to read his lips in order to 'hear' what he was saying.

In any event, work in computer lip-reading – or rather speech-reading, since the computer looks at the person's jaw, tongue, and teeth as well as the lips – has been steadily progressing for more than six years. Why speech-read? To assist with voice recognition, it turns out that combining vision with sound can help a program to distinguish two words that sound similar but look different when they are spoken, like 'me' and 'knee.' Speech reading promises to help for those utterances where acoustic recognition needs it most.

But even assisted speech reading is still in its infancy. Researchers estimate that it will be more than ten years before commercial speech-recognition systems use video cameras to improve their accuracy. Within ten years computers will likely progress to the point where they can get the gist of a conversation by speech reading.

From the moment HAL utters his first words, it is clear to the movie goer that the 9000 series is a superior architecture: HAL's voice is decidedly nonmechanical. For Kubrick, creating HAL's voice was easy. Kubrick simply handed a script containing HAL's words to Douglass Rain, a Shakespearean actor now based in Ontario, Canada, and asked him to read the words into a tape recorder. It took Rain a day and a half. (Three decades later, HAL remains Rain's most memorable role. Perhaps for that reason, the actor refuses to discuss HAL or the film with the press).

After nearly a century's research by scientists trying to produce synthetic speech, Kubrick's technique still dominates the industry. Most games that have 'computer voices,' for example, actually use digitised human speech that has been electronically processed to make it sound more machinelike. Likewise, most computers that speak over the telephone construct what they are trying to say by pasting together phrases from hours of recorded human speech.

Pre-recorded, cut-and-pasted speech works only when there is a limited stock of phrases. But when you need an unlimited collection of phrases and sentences, the only way to produce a computer voice is with synthesised speech.

The biggest users of synthetic speech are the blind. For example, blind people could have this book read to them by DECtalk, a speech synthesiser from Digital

Equipment Corporation. More than ten years old, DECtalk is still one of the best-sounding voice synthesisers on the market. Others could listen to this book on their Macintosh: Apple's System 7.5 come with a speech synthesiser called MacinTalk; an even better synthesiser, MacinTalk Pro, can be downloaded from the company's website.

Listen to HAL's voice and you will discover why synthesising speech is such a hard job. Despite being told to read the words in an emotionless monotone, Rain nevertheless crafted minute timing modulations, pitch shifts, and amplitude changes into the words as he said them. That is because the actor understood the meaning behind the words, and part of that understanding was encoded into those minor variations. He could not help himself.

The way you say something depends on what it means, why you are saying it, and how it relates to what the listener already knows. As a result, much of the research on speech synthesis today has turned into research on understanding natural languages. If you just talk, it is a lot easier than if you have to read aloud something that somebody else wrote. The reason is that when you are talking, you know what you want to say.

Today's computers speak pretty well when they operate within narrow parameters of phrases, but sound mechanical when faced with unrestricted English text. Real breakthroughs will require a better understanding of natural language.

The HAL 9000 comes equipped with a general-purpose video system that follows Poole and Bowman around Discovery. When Poole goes on his spacewalk to replace the AE-35 unit, HAL presumably uses his vision to guide the pod's robotic arm and sever the spacesuit's air hose. Vision systems today are getting very good at tracking people and maintain a pretty good knowledge of where the people are. There are now many face-recognition systems both in the laboratory and the marketplace. These systems cannot pick out a terrorist walking around an airport as seen from a security camera, but they can identify someone using a full-frontal image from a database of a few hundred people. Some can even identify a person turned at an angle.

HAL does more than recognise faces: the computer even has aesthetic sensibilities. When HAL finds Bowman sketching, the computer engages in a conversation about the rendering of the sketch and asks Dave to hold the sketch a bit closer which enables HAL to recognise the sketch to be that of Doctor Hunter.

While artistic appreciation escapes today's computers, a program has been developed that can identify a specific person within a group photograph and another that can recognise objects and faces from line drawings. That program can even say how close the sketch is to a stored template. But none of these systems can do it all. HAL, on the other hand, is a general-purpose intelligence that can understand whatever it sees. For example, HAL realises that Bowman has ventured outside Discovery without his space helmet. That sort of general-purpose recognition is a far more difficult task. It goes beyond image processing and crosses the boundary into common-sense understanding and reasoning about the scene itself – tasks that are beyond today's state of the art.

Today, we can build individual vision systems that perform each of the tasks HAL performs in the film *2001*. But we cannot build a single system that does it all. And we cannot build a system that can handle new and unexpected environments and problems. To achieve that level of sophistication, we need something extra.

The extra something that all of these technologies need to work is natural language understanding and common sense. Indeed, it is these technologies that for many people define the field of AI today. Consider the famous Turing Test, which postulates that a machine will be truly intelligent if you can communicate with it by Teletype and be unable to tell if the machine is a human being or a computer. According to Alan Turing, language skills and common-sense are the essence of intelligence. Turing is famous for his critical part in breaking the German Enigma code during the Second World War and he continued to play a central role in developing the computer as well as being the first to champion AI prior to his tragic death aged 41.

There is just one problem: language understanding and common sense are two things we do not know how to do. Of the two, by far the most work has focused on natural language understanding, or comprehension of language rather than merely the recognition of speech. In the late 1970s, students at Yale University built a computer program called CYRUS, which was programmed to learn everything it could about former US Secretary of State Cyrus Vance by reading the daily newswires. Each time the program read an article about Vance, it would digest the facts of the article and store the information in a conceptual database. You could then ask CYRUS a question in English – say, has your wife ever met the wife of the Prime Minister of Great Britain? The program was actually asked this question and answered, Yes – at a party hosted in Israel.

This led on to a technique called 'case-based reasoning' based on the belief that people have a repertoire of stories they want to tell you. When you ask them a question, it triggers a story. And people use these stories to reason and make decisions about what to do in their lives. This information has been built into a number of corporate training systems, which are really large databanks filled with stories from dozens or even hundreds of people. Got a problem? Ask the computer your question; the machine finds the appropriate story and plays it back to you. The problem with these systems is that using them is like having a conversation with a videodisc player. You get the feeling that no matter what you say; the response was previously recorded – like a low budget daytime television show.

Of course, HAL can clearly do things that these systems are unable to do: HAL is curious. HAL can learn. HAL can create his own plans. It is doubtful that one of the cases programmed into HAL was a recipe for eliminating the crew.

For nearly two decades, other AI researchers have been working on a different approach to teaching computers to learn and understand. They have concluded that almost everything that we would characterise as HAL, that separates HAL from the typical PC running *Windows 2000*, hinges-around this word 'understanding.' It hinges around the totality of common knowledge and common sense and shared knowledge that we humans as a species possess. The differences between HAL and your PC are not a magic program or technique, but a huge 'knowledgebase' filled with rules of thumb, or heuristics, about the world.

HAL would need facts like these to run the ship and care for the crew. And he had needed them to figure out how to dispose of the humans when they started to jeopardise Discovery's mission.

Today there is only one database of common sense in the world. It is Cyc, the core technology used in the products of Cycorp, based in Austin, Texas. Developers have been working on Cyc for more than 13 years. The knowledgebase now contains more than two million bits of assertions. All of the information is arranged in a complicated ontology.

Cyc is making progress in natural language understanding – it can understand commonsensical meanings in written text. Consider these two sentences: "Fred saw the planes flying over Zurich", and "Fred saw the mountains flying over Zurich." Though a conventional parser would say that these sentences are ambiguous, Cyc 'knows' that it is the planes that are doing the flying in the first sentence and Fred who is doing the flying in the second.

Cyc can make these discriminations because the words 'planes' and 'mountains' are more than just plural nouns: they are complex concepts with many associations.

Cyc is already self-aware it knows that it is a computer. If you ask who we are, it knows that we are users. It knows that it is running on a certain machine at a certain place in a certain time. It knows who is talking to it. It knows that a conversation or a run of an application is happening. It has the same kind of time sense that we have. Cyc knows what a computer is and can use that knowledge to answer questions about itself. Like a person, Cyc can perform a chain of reasoning.

But Cyc cannot learn by itself. The developers, or 'ontologizers', have painstakingly entered all of the heuristics in the Cyc knowledgebase as they are called.

The dream is to create a computer program that could learn on its own. Understanding is the key to AI. More than anything else, it is the one technology that eludes science. With true understanding, all of the other AI systems would fall into place. And without it, none of them will ever achieve their potential. Indeed the limitations of logic, some mathematicians say, may be the main reason we do not yet have fully intelligent computers. Traditional approaches to AI assumed that thought could be programmed into computers. Software that can think is on its way, with senses including weight and smell coming sooner to enhance the already available 3D graphics and surround sound.

In the years after the making of *2001*, an interesting rumour began to circulate: HAL's name was a derivation on the computer maker IBM - the letters H, A, and L each coming one letter in the alphabet before the initials I, B, and M. The name was 'adjusted' as IBM felt that the conception HAL projected would damage their own image. Clarke vigorously denied the rumour. The name was not a play on IBM – it was an acronym, of sorts, standing for the words 'heuristic algorithmic'.

Back in the 1960s, heuristics and algorithms were seen as two competing ways of solving the AI puzzle. Heuristics were simple rules of thumb that a computer could apply for solving a problem. Algorithms were direct solutions. HAL presumably used both. Now, thanks to the incredible speed of the computer, a computer can try more variations in a few hours than a human team could attempt in 100 years – a case where humans can learn from machine!

Looking back, the early advances in Artificial Intelligence – for example, teaching computers to play tic-tac-toe and chess – were primarily successes in teaching computers what are essentially artificial skills. Humans are taught how to play chess. And if you can teach somebody how to do something intellectual, you can probably write a computer program to do it as well. I can now solve my crossword more quickly with my Electronic Puzzle Solver. Simply by keying in a ? in place of each unknown letter then the Crossword Puzzle Solver will find every possible match in its word list! It can also find phrases and words by topic. However, this is as far as it can go. It gives a number of choices but it is left to my brain to make 'sense' of the choices and confidently select the correct answer from the other pieces of information in the puzzle.

The problems that haunt AI today are the tasks we cannot program computers to do – largely because we do not know how we do them ourselves. Our lack of understanding about the nature of human consciousness is the reason why there are so few AI researchers working on building it. What does it mean to think? Nobody knows. The real truth is that nobody had a clue how to build an intelligent computer in the 1960s. The same is largely true today.

The hardware that is necessary for what HAL has is available today. It is organisation, software, structure, programming, and learning that we do not have right yet. That is a lot of substance. And it is a dramatic ideological reversal from the 1960s, when AI researchers were sure that solutions to the most vexing problems of the mind were just around the corner. Back then, researchers thought the only things they lacked were computers fast enough to run their algorithms and heuristics. Sooner or later, we will build a computer that can think and learn and talk, but it is unlikely to be based on current silicon chip technology. Silicon microprocessors, no matter how fast they become at performing instructions are really little more than lumps of logic. It deals only with concepts like on or off, true or false and has no truck with vague possibilities. But silicon is not the only material that can be used to build logical devices. Currently under investigation is the plan to make biological cells programmable like processors. The aim is to mimic the workings of the logic gates in silicon microprocessors inside the cell. Cells contain a material that has several advantages over silicon. It has been debugged for far longer than silicon, is used in far more computational devices than silicon and it is very easy to reproduce. The material is DNA. DNA coupled with natural selection is unbeatable when it comes to preserving information. For example the cluster of genes called hox tells the cells of an embryo where they are on the body so they know what to grow into, be it legs, lungs or lymph nodes. Hox first appeared around three billion years ago and has been quietly doing the same job the same way generation after generation.

The cult sci-fi series, *Star Trek* can be seen as a melting pot of sci-fi imaginations in the 1960s. During the writing of the series, Gene Roddenberry was supported by Samuel Peeples. He was also influenced by a number of other sci-fi writers including Robert Bloch, Frederic Brown, Nelson Bond, Richard Matheson, Howard Brown, Pohl Anderson, Theodore Sturgeon, Jerry Sohl and James E. Gunn. *Star Trek* chronicled the adventures of eight principal characters: Captain James Kirk; Mr Spock, the science officer, born of a Vulcanian father and Earthling mother; Lieutenant Uhura, the communications officer; 'Scotty', or Montgomery Scott, the chief engineer; Dr Leonard 'Bones' McCoy, the medical officer; Mr. Sulu, the helmsman; Christine Chapel, the chief nurse and Ensign Pavel Chekov, the navigator. The 78 episodes traced the crew's mission to 'seek out new life and new civilisations', and along the way they encountered all environments and a variety of intelligent life-forms, from gaseous beings to humanoids. I think *Star Trek* might be seen as giving us an insight into what the *Alien Visitor* was like and the kind of space travel we might achieve in the future. Unlike the other novels and films I have mentioned, *Star Trek* suggests our space travel is not limited to the moon which is comparatively close to Earth. It seems from the series that we may be able to travel through many galaxies. The optimism of the series shows space travel can be a good thing. It also introduced ideas such as lasers and materialisation and de-materialisation. If Star Trek somehow does tap into our *Alien Visitor* memory perhaps we can understand why the *Alien Visitor* came to Earth. Perhaps the journey to the planet was part of a fact-finding mission.

Some ideas – put forward by sci-fi writers – have become so well known that they are part of the general consciousness. Flying Saucers have been in our imaginations for decades. There are even attempts to build aircraft based on the notion of a flying saucer. A low-cost spacecraft, called *Lightcraft,* which is shaped like a flying saucer, is in the design stage.

A further interesting group, which over the centuries have provided spectacular 3-D visual insights into their imaginations, are architects. What did they 'see' in their imagination to inspire buildings such as St Paul's Cathedral, Taj Mahal, Sydney Opera House, the Empire State building, Eiffel Tower to name but a few?

Imagination is not only the domain of the Sc-fi writers and architects - it applies to all of us.

I think that even though we may gain some flashes of our *Alien Visitor* memories we have problems deciphering them. Just as the original function of Silbury Hill, the pyramids and Stonehenge remain a mystery to us so do some of our memories. It could be argued that following the destruction of the original *Alien Visitor* civilisation, a wealth of information about this visitor could have been recorded and kept by our ancestors. Perhaps it was even placed in sanctuaries for study and safe-keeping which we might find one day. However, without this information today, it is hard to provide a context for these memories. It may be that all our different religions are fragments of one religion of the *Alien Visitor* and that religious ideas and visions are related to this one huge faith. What remains today of the *Alien Visitor's* faith may be these complicated and abstracted ideas in our mind and interpretations made by people through the generations which have been handed down and committed to text. However, these may be corrupted versions of very ancient ideas that founded all our cultures, as I believe we are all related to the *Alien Visitor*.

I am convinced the way we will finally uncover and understand this *Alien Visitor* memory is by pooling our ideas. As I have said earlier, we may well be networked together by the common gene, so it seems inevitable that we will be able to share our knowledge. We have already advanced from communicating by word of mouth, through various art forms, to writing followed by the mass production of books, then photography, telecommunication, films, radio TV, video and video conferencing. Today we can communicate to millions of people all over the world on TV via satellites but significantly, with the massive advances in telecommunication and computer products we can now interact with each other. The size of the world is perhaps shrinking with the concept of cyberspace as communications technology enables us to learn more about the world and all the different kinds of people in it. With the advent of websites we can share our ideas with thousands of people rather than just our families, friends and neighbours. The only qualification for joining the net is that you are alive. Information that was once confined to the private space of an individual brain becomes shared in cyberspace. I believe that the net will grow in size with more and more people contributing to it from around the world. Eventually we will build up a database of information comparable with the size of the *Alien Visitor's* knowledge. As computers become more sophisticated, our ability to share our ideas will increase thus bringing more and more of the knowledge in our *Alien Visitor* memory to light. Microprocessors have already grown from a thousand transistors per silicon chip in the early Seventies, to currently 100 million and heading towards 300 million transistors per chip and with much more to come. Computer memories have leapt in storage density from a few thousand bytes to gigabytes, terabytes and heading towards yottabytes of information.

In 1969, there were four computers on the fledgling internet. Today there are more than 40 million internet users and this figure is going up all the time. There are already more than one billion personal computers being used in the world today. It is predicted that in the near future the number of personal computers sold throughout the world, in a single year, will exceed one billion. The term 'personal computer' includes computers incorporated into televisions, games systems and robots. Computers will continue to make rapid advances and steps towards a 'quantum computer' is already being developed by computer companies. This supercomputer is referred to as 'quantum' because it will have capabilities that are a huge leap forward from those produced by existing technology. Corporations such as IBM, Hewlett Packard, Intel and Microsoft are already conceiving products many years ahead. Nevertheless, these super logic computers still have a long way to go to compete with human intuition – our 'gut feeling'.

The world wide web is, in my view, the most significant innovation of the twentieth century. The key to the net is that it is a connection system between millions of computers and hence millions of human minds. The power of the net is that it lies beyond the control of its users, companies or nations – and you cannot switch it off! Like roads, railways and telephones, the net brings a hitherto inconceivable level of connectivity to the world. It has the potential to make the world a smaller place with a greater chance for the sharing of ideas with more people of all cultures. The internet brings freedom to explore our imagination through contact with millions of people. This book comes with a website and I hope that it will open up a sharing of ideas. The site is at **www.silburydawning,com** with the email address *feedback@silburydawning.com* The interactive nature of the net – which already encompasses video conferencing and satellite communication technology – could help us to trace our roots. We can find out if we are related to people on the other side of the world, with incredible variations in the lifestyles. This chance to pool data could lead to scientists sharing more information and statistics which could result in more inventions and cures for diseases. This pooling of data will help us to draw out and comprehend our hidden memories so those things that seem inexplicable and perhaps frightening or irrational may be explained. Perhaps, everything that we class as supernatural will gradually become more understood.

I believe, ironically, we will be able to uncover our *Alien Visitor* memory using the computer which we have attempted to model on our own brains and intelligence. It is with this man-made tool that we will discover our *Alien Visitor* heritage. But I also believe that without this *Alien Visitor* gene we would not have been able to build computers. By creating computers, we have already started to use our *Alien Visitor* capabilities to find out all we are capable of and to learn more about our alien ancestors.

Chapter 13

THE END OF THE BEGINNING

I firmly believe that around 13,000 years ago there was a higher level of intelligent life on our planet than there is today. I feel we are still struggling to understand how or why the great achievements of this time were made, such as Silbury Hill or the pyramids. The proof of the *Alien Visitor's* time on Earth seems to be lost but myths and legends which have so much in common despite coming from the four corners of the Earth persist. Perhaps these are distorted accounts of this time in our early history. These stories have remained as if determined to stick it out until we understand their significance and start to understand them as true chronicles, rather than fictional or allegorical stories.

Just as religions across the world started to offer us insights into who we are and where we come from, Darwin told us we were descended from the first animals to inhabit the planet. I believe we are descended from apes but also; we are descended from a race which, at the moment, we only know through mythology. We are starting to look into these myths and wonder if they may describe a civilisation that pre-dates those we have discovered so far. We are also capable of travelling not only above but also out of our own planet and we can visit and monitor neighbouring planets. We are confident that one day in the near future we will be able to live on the moon and visit faraway stars.

Can there be any doubt that the progress of the human race is due to the legacy left by the *Alien Visitor*? By using inventions, such as the internet, we will find more ways to communicate our ideas and to open up conversations to include people from all over the world. The old saying tells us 'two heads are better than one' but what could millions of heads come up with, sharing their ideas on the world wide web. Will we be able to jointly piece together our thoughts to return to the high level of individual intelligence which the *Alien Visitor* once brought to this planet and passed down to us? I firmly believe our use of more and more advanced communication technology is the key to reaching our legacy. Through the use of our combined minds and imaginations we can discover what the *Alien Visitor* was and what it accomplished. If we find a way of unlocking our subconscious memory and potential for genius from the *Alien Visitor* and sharing it with each other, we will be able to answer these questions. More than this, these achievements will become our future. We need to look not just for the physical remains of the *Alien Visitor* in Egypt but also for the remains of its memory and genius in ourselves.

Are we now on the brink of the next phase of our remarkable evolution?

It is clear that we have moved from a time when man must be told what to do, to a new beginning where man will slowly learn the truth and be able to think for himself. The ideological shift is enormous and it is occurring right now.

As communications increase between people who would have never spoken to each other before, are we now in a position to understand each other and pool all our knowledge? Our use of a common language is spreading. We can tell each other how to avoid collisions at sea or in the air and are finding ways of entering more complicated dialogue using rapidly evolving computer and communication technology which translates conversations as they take place.

Since the departure of the *Alien Visitor* from our planet, we have been confused about who we are and have looked towards the skies for an answer. Without something beyond this world, beyond ourselves, we have been unable to create the social structures in which a person can truly be a person. As a result, I think people developed strong beliefs in different religions over the centuries. But now I feel there is evidence of the loosening of religious structures in our lives and some of these beliefs are being strongly questioned. In the case of the Church of England, only two per cent of the population regularly attends services. I believe all these different faiths in a power greater than ourselves are all expressions of a desire to know where we come from. But I do not think the answer is a nebulous god but a real ancestor who lived on our planet – the *Alien Visitor*.

Ever since we gained the *Alien Visitor* gene and memory, we have been unconsciously aware of another home away from Earth. I suspect a hidden homesickness or curiosity about this home is the driving force behind our interest in space travel and fascination with what lies beyond our planet. Without the technology and the knowledge to return 'home', we have tried to find the answer to our questions about where we come from in a number of religions. Some have turned to a Catholic church, others an English chapel, a Scottish kirk, a Buddhist temple, a Shinto shrine, a synagogue or a mosque.

Perhaps the sharing of our knowledge is taking us to a point in the near future where we will be able to penetrate further into space and maybe find out more about other life-forms, maybe even find our ancestors.

I hope that we will be able to achieve the potential that our *Alien Visitor* gene has given us and that we will not perish as a race before we have done this. One threat to our survival is a war. Ironically, it is because of our *Alien Visitor* gene that we have a tendency to war. We are more aggressive than any of our nearest relatives in the animal kingdom and have employed our intelligence to create weapons of destruction and torture. I feel this is, sadly, the downside of us all possessing a gene with super-intelligence. Perhaps initially the *Alien Visitor* was able to control our ancestors but as the *Alien Visitor* gene found its way into the general population, this intelligence led to conflicts. This kind of situation is explained well by Edward Gall in his published lecture 'The Mystery of Satan'[30]:

In the earlier human races of which Theosophy tells us, man had not yet developed the power of Self-determination and Free-will. He lived and evolved under the direct 'guidance' and inspiration of the great semi-divine Kings, who were also Priest-Initiates, beings who had passed through their purely human stages of evolution in earlier Cycles and who had now incarnated to

---

[30] Edward Gall - The Blavatsky Lecture 1973 Extract from *The Mystery of Satan*
Printed by Reg Sharpe

help the main body of the people who were still in the earlier stages of their human evolution. In no sense whatever were the people of the time self-dependent, self-determining beings. The Royal Initiates took the lead and guided, in every way, the people merely followed.

I think the *Alien Visitors* were the first 'great, semi-divine Kings' but as the masses gained greater intelligence, as the gene was propagated, they started to gain 'self-determination and freewill' and a desire to gain knowledge rather than carry out mundane tasks. We have records from the ancient world which describe revolutionaries who question authority and dissatisfaction with leaders. The stories in the Bible about Moses and Jesus present them as revolutionary in this way. Moses leads his people out of one civilisation to find their own land and Jesus encourages people to believe in their own individuality, regardless of their social standing which is defined by the Roman society. I am not necessarily suggesting that Moses and Jesus were some of these first revolutionaries in *Alien Visitor* societies but rather that the reports about them may have been influenced by earlier reports about such revolutionaries. For example, no one would suggest that King Arthur was Jesus but the way that Arthur gathers his knights for his round table is similar to the way that Jesus gathers his disciples. In this way, the myths about King Arthur can be seen to incorporate ideas from earlier reports that have also become myths.

Herodotus recorded the reign of Pharaoh Khufu and his son Khafre and said between them they caused 106 years of oppression and misery. An army was created to protect them and uphold the rules in their state. The evolution of this aggression, gained from greater self-determination, can be seen to be behind violent attempts to create states by armies. In this way, the army is not a product of a state but the state is the product of the army's desire to flaunt its aggression. Even armies have been challenged, from within, by individual soldiers who have become mercenaries. The end of the Cold War and moves by the world's most powerful countries to reduce their number of nuclear weapons is a positive sign that we are trying, in some parts of the world, to prevent war with some other countries. Nevertheless, conflicts in Afghanistan, Bosnia, Chechnya, Kosovo, and Rwanda, the irrational behaviour of dictators like Slobodan Milosevic in Yugoslavia, Sadam Hussein in Iraq, Colonel Muammar Gadaffi in Libya, Osama bin Laden in Afghanistan, the nuclear arms race between India and Pakistan and the rise in terrorist martyrdom, show how rife and complex this desire to war can be. There is no doubt that we have the ability to regress our civilisation by thousands of years either by means of a nuclear holocaust or man-made plague. There are fears that we could even wipe out the world's population in a global nuclear war. I hope we will be able to control this desire to war in order to achieve the positive gifts of the gene.

There are also external events which could prevent us from fully realising our legacy from the *Alien Visitor*. The stability of our existence and that of our planet cannot be guaranteed. The catastrophe which the *lystrosaur* survived is one of many such events we are aware of to strike Earth, the last obliterating the dinosaurs. These events took away 90 per cent of the species that were alive at those times. Scientists believe that within a few hundred years as many as 99 per cent of all species of animals that have lived on Earth will be extinct. Whole forests will fall silent. The nightingale, which is the subject of so many English songs, verse and prose, is rapidly vanishing from Britain and could be facing extinction. There are now probably more representations of nightingales in English literature than there are actually birds. While most Britons have never heard a nightingale sing, its vocal ability has been admired in the work of Chaucer, Milton, Keats and Shakespeare. Keats may have been wrong when he wrote: "Thou was not born for death, immortal bird!" Man will not be able to compensate for the benefits that other species, including the smallest single-celled marine plants and bacteria, contribute to the stability of the Earth's ecosystem.

Another threat to our existence is a disease or virus that could either by accident or design render us extinct. The worst virus in recent times in the so-called Spanish Flu pandemic that killed around 25 million people worldwide between 1918 and 1919 – this is a greater number of deaths than those caused by World War One. Superbugs which seem to be able to resist all our antibiotics are prevalent today. Since the late 1970s, the HIV virus has spread across the world, killing huge numbers of people in every country, particularly Africa. There is much about this virus that still perplexes our scientists and we currently have no cure for it although drugs to delay the breakdown of the immune system are becoming more sophisticated. However, they are not always available in places where the virus is most common. So, it is a distinct probability that future 'flu virus pandemics from unforeseen origins will be inevitable.

The likelihood of us being struck by an asteroid in the future is highly probable. According to the

International Astronomical Union, an asteroid capable of destroying human civilisation is due to pass very close to Earth – possibly within the moon's orbit – on Thursday October 23 2028. However, NASA estimates that the asteroid – which is known as 1997 XFII – will pass 600,000 miles away from Earth, instead of the 30,000 miles previously calculated. A newer asteroid, the 1998 DK36 is likely to miss Earth by 750,000 miles. But this does not rule out asteroids which we have not yet spotted or of which we have no warning. The Earth has already been struck by large meteors, as testified by the Meteor Crater in Arizona. In 1908, a comet exploded and the fallout of this landed near Lake Tunguska in Siberia. No one was killed, but if it had exploded half an hour earlier it would have obliterated St Petersburg.

The depletion of the planet's resources could also threaten our survival as a race. Today, according to United Nations calculations, there are now more than six billion people on our planet needing a share of fuel, water and food. The World Energy Council predicts that in 30 years' time, the world's energy demands will have doubled. Meanwhile, oil and gas – although not necessarily coal – will have all but vanished. Our inventions, such as rockets or hairspray, are increasing pollution. Scientists have observed that about five miles of sky have been lost since 1958. Some rockets puncture holes measuring up to four miles wide in the world's protective ozone layer, posing a threat to the stratosphere. Our skies are constantly criss-crossed with thousands of jet planes. Climate changes due to global warming are evident in all parts of the world. The weather phenomenon, El Niño – which is caused by the rising temperature of the Pacific Ocean – has unleashed some of the worst weather of this century with floods in South America, devastating downpours in California, ice storms in Canada and droughts in Africa. Conversely, an abnormally low temperature of the ocean – which is called La Niña – has altered currents, trade winds and climate. It is even believed that the powerful changes caused by El Niño and La Niña have slightly slowed down the speed at which the Earth rotates.

We need to try to make sure our planet is healthy enough for us to live in so we can continue our development. I believe that where we can control changes on the planet – such as our population, which in turn will reduce levels of pollution or the decline or certain species – we should do our best to protect our future.

A subtler way in which we may also be preventing ourselves from uncovering our *Alien gene* is our adherence to ideologies that may be opposed to the information which this gene can give us. For example, if we are trying to interpret our *Alien Visitor* memories in the context of political or religious ideas – which are opposed to the idea of democratic intelligence – then we will not be encouraged to draw out our abilities. My point is that all our ideologies, the world over and throughout time, has their seed in the *Alien Visitor* culture. Therefore, to fully understand this culture which we hold in our memories we need to understand all these ideologies. This is difficult because they can be contradictory and one ideology will often forbid another. Throughout history, certain political or religious leaders have attempted to obscure other ideologies in order to gain power over a group of people. For example, during the Russian Revolution, the Communists gained support for their ideas by stirring up hatred for the monarchy. The Communists wanted to rule Russia and it was not in their interests to contend with other ideologies that they felt would challenge their own. They wanted to persuade the majority of people to follow them and did this by turning them against the minority of more wealthy people. The same thing can be said to have happened during the French Revolution and in Hitler's Germany. Any system that is so imposing that it does not allow for fresh ideas could hold back or even prevent our race understanding all it is capable of. Appreciating our uniqueness can help in resolving misunderstandings and conflicts both personal and social. If we are truly to pool all our intelligence together we need to be extremely tolerant and make sure we do not ostracise people who are good at expressing their intelligence and can encourage other people to use their intelligence too. This is why I trust the internet may be our best chance of pooling this knowledge, because it is not controlled by any group and rather invites a sharing of ideas. With this rapidly improving computer technology we may one day be able to reconstruct the position of Earth in the heavens 10,000 to 13,000 years ago. I hope we will also devise the technology to enable us to set off for these places to find out more about where we came from. I think we will learn how to use the *Alien Visitor's* form of Yoga to unravel the secrets of the Silbury Hill complex and those similar structures which can be found in many other parts of the world, and the associated crop circle formations.

Perhaps the stone structures close to Silbury Hill are encoded with data in a similar way to how we store information on pieces of silicon or aluminium alloy platters, coated with a thin, magnetic film in our computer/television systems. This information is not visible but might be accessible by tapping into ley line 'frequencies'. We might be able to decipher the meaning of these structures using Yoga, which also taps into this kind of energy. When we work out how to find this flow of energy at the right 'frequency', we will be able to 'log on' to the complex to find out where our ancestor came from or in which direction it was heading when it left us.

With the destruction of these megaliths over the centuries has the data been lost? I believe not. We have inherited the *Alien Visitor* knowledge and we are also storing this data. We collectively have this information in our brains and we now have the ability, not only to put our ideas 'down on paper' in many tons of books, but we can now compress much more information onto computer hard disks - millions of them!

But I believe we could also find the proof of an *Alien Visitor* heritage using our evolving science and archaeological finds. I am convinced our fascination with genetic science linked with an analysis of the mummified remains of our oldest existing ancestors holds the key to confirming the presence of the *Alien Visitor* gene and hence the arrival of the *Alien Visitor* on our planet. We can investigate the many 'natural' mummies, which have been preserved for thousands of years in ice or peat bogs. And there are thousands of the embalmed mummies from Egypt and elsewhere, many still waiting to be discovered. Further study of them will reveal the subtle changes in the *Homo* species to the growth of the human. We will eventually be able to invent the technology to look specifically for the *Alien Visitor* DNA in these mummies to confirm who we are and live up to all we can achieve.

I firmly believe that in spite of the fact that we have inherited these memory genes from our ancestors, predominantly from the *Alien Visitor*, we are still in control of the development of our knowledge and our destiny under the prevailing conditions on Earth. Like accessing the Hard Disk Drive (HDD) in the computer to retrieve a file that we can alter before returning to the HDD, so we can do exactly the same thing with the data in our brain.

But, the inheritance of the *Alien Visitor* gene under the prevailing conditions on Earth has a serious weakness that has hampered our recovery through ignorance, intolerance and war. It has created an ego in some individuals who use their knowledge, gained from the gene, to their advantage.

It is very important to recognise that ironically, the more knowledge we recover, the more bigoted and intolerant we can become. But we must settle our differences, as there is so much of the world and the universe for future generations to explore. We do not necessarily need to make the same mistakes as our ancestors, provided we pay attention to our evolving knowledge and discoveries. For example, the simple concept of heaven and hell has had a huge negative influence on mankind through the centuries in the name of religion. Unshackling ourselves from what we now realise is a ridiculous idea will have an immense effect on our ability to think for ourselves.

Epigenetics may provide us with the science to explore our trans-generational memory genes to re-discover our history in much greater detail than had hitherto seemed possible. Understanding our 'real' history may confirm our alien heritage and help us on the path to universal love.

I wonder if the *Alien Visitor* is aware that it had inadvertently left its knowledge and experiences behind on our planet. So is the *Alien Visitor* planning to return to Earth? At present humankind is not ready to accept the *Alien Visitor* without extreme confrontation. So, it is very unlikely to make itself known to the masses for quite some time unless we approach the point of self-destruction of planet Earth. The *Alien Visitor* would not allow this to happen because of the far-reaching catastrophic effects this would have on other civilizations throughout the universe. The universe can only exist in harmony – so why should we fear the *Alien Visitor*?

I believe that before the *Alien Visitor* can revisit the human race must remove the shackles of mass manipulation of our desires, as clearly demonstrated by the tobacco and snack industries and develop an individual and collective understanding at a subconscious level, of compassion, kindness (love in action), peace and harmony. We must invest in ourselves – in the physical and the spiritual! It is therefore important that we keep ourselves in harmony to become a complete person.

When we believe that someone else has our best interests at heart we are enveloped in feelings of contentment and well-being. So, conversely, we must also be aware, and also understand, that our own mental actions and thoughts towards others have a comparable effect.

Buddhists are taught that it is well worthwhile practising and developing 'metta' or 'loving kindness' meditation. The development of a mind full of universal love and friendliness towards our self and all other beings is a very powerful mediation and the influence and practical effect of this meditation should never be underestimated. Developing 'metta' means letting go of negative states of mind and this, in turn, makes room for positive thoughts and positive states of mind. Alan James says in his book, [31]*Inner Tranquillity;*

"Success in loving-kindness mediation is marked by a growing absence of annoyance. You become more easy-going, tolerant and are more often than not, likely to give others the benefit of the doubt."

Loving kindness motivates us to behave kindly to all beings at all times and to speak gently in their presence and in their absence. This positive mental state and optimistic outlook gives rise to a sense of oneness and interconnectedness with all beings.

If our practice is sincere and heartfelt then it is never mere sentiment and emotion or just words with no consequences. Our thoughts of loving kindness - that we wish all beings to be friendly and never hostile, happy and never unhappy, to enjoy well-being and never be distressed, are significant and will have beneficial results and outcomes both for them and for us.

Convincing politicians, monarchists, captains of industry, religious leaders and other egotists that we as individuals are more than capable of looking after ourselves and the safekeeping of our precious planet and that we would all be better off when 'society' ceases to exist, is a long way away. But we must begin NOW for the safety of our planet (and all its life forms) and its

---

[31] James, Alan   *Inner Tranquillity*   Aukana Trust 2002

future within the universe. The tragic events in New York on September 11 confirm my comments above. When we all turn into ourselves this engenders in us at a collective subconscious level the senses of compassion, kindness, peace and harmony immediately following such a tragedy. For example, crime almost disappeared in America when 'society' ceased to exist following the tragic events of September 11, albeit for a brief period of time, before mass manipulation kicks in again.

But help from the *Alien Visitor* is already on its way in different guises. For example I believe that crop formations provoke a mind enhancing experience by getting us as individuals to throw back into ourselves. This is a subtle way of getting each and every one of us to explore our amazing subconscious which will enable us to return our collective minds to the time when the *Alien Visitor* arrived on our planet thus creating the conditions of compassion, love, peace and harmony, for the safe and welcome return of the *Alien Visitor(s)*.

When it returns or we ever find it, I believe we will have some common knowledge that will enable us to understand the secrets of space and our hidden powers? Will we then fulfil the purpose of our lives and our place in the universe?

LIVING BOOK TIMELINE

My book has taken me on an incredible journey since it was first published in 2000.

In this 20th Anniversary Edition of the book I wanted to tell the story of how it attracted opportunities and ideas and evolved. I wanted to more fully acknowledge all those who provided me with feedback and inspiration and opportunities because it feels to me as if this book has had a life after its first publication. So, I've created what I call a Living Book Timeline.

Spring 2000

Early adoption of self-publishing

During writing the book I was living in Wiltshire (which houses Stonehenge, Avebury, Stanton Drew and Silbury Hill) where many local people, and visitors from all over the world, are seeking to find answers to these ancient constructions. I became desperate to get my ideas out and share them with them. I realised a great way of reaching these already-interested audiences would be to put the book where they could find it. So, I took the decision to self-publish. The Henge Shop, located in Avebury, Wiltshire, is within walking distance of Silbury Hill and it became the first location to sell lots of copies of my book. I am grateful for the help from the owners of *The Henge Shop* Phillipe and Dominque Ullens.

In the days before CreateSpace, Kindle Direct Publishing, and very user-friendly and code-free content management systems, this involved creating an independent publishing company (which I called *The Media Shack*) and directly approaching national and international booksellers. From the outset I was intrigued to find that what I thought of as a very niche book was sold by mainstream booksellers including Barnes and Noble and Waterstones.

Seeing this wider interest spurred me on to find opportunities to sell the book online enlisting help from local website expert George Brown at *Insight Global* his generous support working together on this project has been very much valued.

An incredible coincidence!

Almost at the same time I published my book, attempting to delve into the secrets of Silbury Hill, the Hill itself opened up. On the 29 May 2000, after heavy rains, a collapse of the 1776 vertical shaft dug by Edward Drax (with Cornish miners) in 1776 produced a gaping hole on the summit of Silbury Hill in Wiltshire.

When the hole first appeared Dutch crop circle enthusiasts, Bert Janssen and Janet Ossebaard abseiled down the shaft and filmed some interesting discoveries - smooth walls and sharp corners indicating the presence of a chamber inside the hill and significant levels of electrostatic electricity which destroyed a mobile phone which had been accidentally carried down into the shaft.

This experience captured on their film *The Silbury Hole Enigma* confirmed my belief that Silbury Hill was something more than a chalk heap.

Following this incident, English Heritage decided to plan for a Silbury Hill Restoration and Conservation project in 2008 (see further on in Timeline).

November 2001 -May 2006

Speaking opportunities

My instinct to publish the book locally was a good one because it brought me into direct contact with other people fascinated by unexplained mysteries in Wiltshire and beyond.

Due to growing local awareness of the book, I was invited to speak at my first conference called *Mysteries of the World 2001*, in Marlborough, Wiltshire. Marlborough is just 6 miles from Avebury, the internationally regarded hub of British crop-circle appearances.

Speakers at the conference included Reg Presley, leader of 1960s group The Troggs and a respected Ufologist.

Also speaking was Polly Carson, the Alton Barnes farmer whose land has featured some of the most spectacular formations in the area.

And for conference-goers more interested in conspiracy theories, author Jon King spoke about the death of Diana, Princess of Wales.

I'm grateful to Kerry Jean McKenna, an enthusiastic event organiser who started my journey into public speaking. This led to fantastic opportunities to exchange ideas with other speakers and delegates who included Graham Hancock and Robert Bauval.

September 2002

Second edition of Silbury Dawning published

The website, speaking opportunities and interviews on radio and television meant the book attracted a lot of interesting feedback and ideas which I wanted to incorporate. So I added a further chapter called *Imagination* and published the book in a second edition.

What astounded me was that this feedback was no longer just coming from a local, interested audience but from beyond Wiltshire, then the UK and Europe. As sales and feedback came in from other continents, it felt to me that the book itself was tapping into the very 'collective unconscious' I had written about in the first edition. However, I was starting to see that this collective unconscious was a much larger force than I had imagined. It seemed to me that the growth of the internet, was making it easier for the book to reach into a worldwide collective unconsciousness. Other people, who perhaps shared little in terms of lifestyle or geography with me, made contact with information and ideas which seemed to me to reinforce that what we did all have in common was a shared fascination with this point of origin for our intelligence. I wanted the book to capture this exciting wider thinking.

May 2006

A good conversation

A growing interest in the number of crop circles appearing in Wiltshire led to the creation of the Silent Circle Café in Cherhill near Calne, by Charles Mallett, a great place to meet and discuss ideas about them and other mysterious phenomenon in the county. Charles kindly supported my book and his knowledge of crop circles is second to none with an incredibly informative *The Croppie* website. There are hoaxes, but Charles looks at those which are difficult to explain.

Another valuable contact for the book, who I met at the café, was professional dowser Maria Wheatley from nearby Avebury. She provided valuable information on energies surrounding the Avebury stone circles and megaliths from her worldwide investigations. She regularly shares her ideas and research on social media.

I enjoyed sharing my ideas with Charles and Maria, and at the café, that Silbury Hill and other structures such as Stonehenge may have at some time in the past been a form of energy source, a transmitting/receiving device or an early universal WIFI network using ley lines.

2007 to 2008

The secrets of Silbury Hill unearthed

In 2007 English Heritage commissioned a major programme of conservation and renovation work to stabilise Silbury Hill. This project provided a unique opportunity to find out more about this ancient monument. Atkinson's 1968 tunnel was reopened, giving archaeologists a final opportunity to record the inside of Silbury Hill.

Local journalist Nigel Kerton took a keen interest in promoting my book in the *Gazette and Herald* and my work at Silbury Hill. This relationship enabled me to gain access to the Atkinson's tunnel to gather information and take me to the centre of Silbury hill during English Heritage's project.

Much of the information recorded by English Heritage archaeologists is stored in at the National Oceanography Centre at Southampton University, for future people to study.

An excellent book followed the project, *The Story of Silbury Hill*, including a foreword from David Attenborough.

For me, this incredibly fortuitous opportunity to access the Hill helped me think about it from the perspective of my own book. I found myself disagreeing with some of the interpretations of the findings and this triggered me to create my own theory which became Chapter Six, *Pyramids*, of this book and a spin-off leaflet exploring my alternative theory about the construction of Silbury Hill as described in the book.

August 2008

Pyramids in Bosnia

I was invited to the *First International Scientific Conference: Bosnian Valley of the Pyramids in Sarajevo*, as a guest by Dr Sam Osmanagich who had read my book, to give my presentation titled 'Silbury Hill - The White Pyramid?' The paper presented my recent findings at Silbury Hill.

I met distinguished Egyptologists, archaeologists, physicists, chemists, geologists, academics and independent researchers from Europe, US, Russia and

China eager, like me, to investigate newly discovered pyramids.

It also became evident that many like-minded and open-minded delegates were keen to share their research and explore the many aspects of the ancient pyramid phenomenon.

The weeklong conference provided further first-hand evidence for hundreds of mounds similar to Silbury Hill throughout the world! It also provided the catalyst to compare the recent findings at Silbury Hill with those from other pyramids. This further expanded the new Chapter 6.

September 2009

Egypt Tour

It was inevitable perhaps that I would visit Egypt!

Kate Fenn, who I had met after one of my talks, invited me to join her wonderful group because of our shared archaeological interest in pyramids and my general thirst for independent research.

She is trained in Egyptology and Archaeology, Health and Social Care, combining her healing and spiritual paths to help raise awareness, consciousness and stimulate healing through the use of meditation, sweat lodge ceremonies, vision quest healing, and the Medicine Wheel traditions around the globe.

The trip involved an excursion down the Nile from Alexandria to Luxor with trios to various temples and pyramids and the incredible experience of camping out in the Sahara Desert beneath the canopy of the stars of the Milky Way in all its glory due to zero light pollution.

Some of the key ideas which helped me developed the book and came from my fellow travellers were regarding energies all around us.

Two experiences which had a great impact on me, and the book happened here. The first was seeing a pyramid of the same size as Silbury Hill next to the so-called Bent Pyramid on the Giza Plateau some 40 kilometres south of Cairo.

This increased my conviction that Silbury Hill had originally been constructed as a pyramid and my ideas are in Chapter 6.

The climax of the trip was gaining privileged access to a subterranean chamber, 30 meters beneath the Great Pyramid. Very few get access to this chamber. Crouching here I felt profoundly that this technologically complex structure was originally constructed for the purposes of energy and life rather than as a tomb for the dead.

2009-present

Beyond the Website

With the growth of social media and mass communication channels I was keen to make sure the book and my ideas were not just confined to my own website and forum on the site. I started contributing articles to *Ezine* and inviting feedback there.

July 2013

Glastonbury Symposium

I was invited to give a lecture at the internationally renowned Glastonbury Symposium by the main organiser Andy Thomas who was aware of my various talks on Silbury Hill and felt my talk would be very relevant to his conference.

Andy is a leading researcher into mysteries and cover-ups and is the author of the acclaimed *The Truth Agenda* and *Conspiracies,* both widely praised for providing real insights into classic conspiracy theories and the paranormal.

The Symposium's remit is to promote 'Truth, Mysteries and New Frontiers'.

My lecture explores how the very first pyramids were built on every continent on Earth using knowledge which we name quantum physics today.

I believe this knowledge of energy at a sub-atomic level originated from our ancient ancestors. In my lecture I explain the original purpose of the pyramids was not for death, as tombs for the dead. Although this may have been how they were later used.

But rather their original purpose was for sustaining and promoting life for the *alien visitor* and the society it was building for the future on Earth.

My interpretation of the pyramids and their relation to the concept of the Afterlife was that they were for the ongoing survival of a post-*alien visitor* species, rather than the passing of privileged individuals into another world.

The lecture goes on to focus on Silbury Hill as an early pyramid, designed to generate or even create electricity from a water source identified at its base.

Much of this was introduced into the book in Chapter 6 and the lecture can be viewed on YouTube where it has attracted thousands of views.

I believe recovery of this sort of technology would be hugely useful in our current quest to find new energy sources.

August 2014

The First Bases Project Conference

I was invited to give a talk at *The First Bases Project Conference*, organised by Miles Johnston, which took place at Marlborough College in Wiltshire. The conference theme was 'Humanity is Changing'.

My presentation was titled 'Silbury Hill: At the Dawning of Humanity' and it has attracted thousands of views on *YouTube*..

May 2014

First podcast

I wanted to get involved in new opportunities to podcast and my journey into this new format with the book started with the award-winning *Lifting the Veil* with Abbie Dent on SoundartRadio 102.5FM.

June 2016

Pyramids in Menorca

The island of Menorca has a large number of pyramids and stone megaliths so I was eager to visit it. A great opportunity arose to go there with the same group with which I had visited Egypt in 2009. I saw first-hand the reach of the *alien visitors'* technology and civilisation. It went far beyond Egypt or Wiltshire as I had originally suggested in the book.

April 2019

Broadcasting both sides of the Atlantic

I was invited to speak about my *alien visitor* gene theory by broadcasters in the UK and US. I was interviewed by Naz Ahsun on Swindon 105.5 *Outer Limits* radio programme and with the US-based *Mack Maloney*, Military X-Files and *Michael Vara* from WCET.FM.

Later in the year I was interviewed on *BBS TV* - a worldwide digital live broadcaster.

Today, Spring 2020

It is a great deal easier to self-publish and sell a book today than it was 20 years ago which can only be a good thing as it gives more people more opportunities to share their ideas and connect with others, creating their own 'living books'.

My hope for this 20th Anniversary of my book is that it will continue to thrive in the world and to help current and future generations access our intelligent inheritance to solve and exceed the challenges which may feel overwhelming to us today. I am confident we can when we see the acceleration of our desire to communicate in the last 20 years alone.

Could this recovery of knowledge resolve today's challenges? I strongly believe it will.

First Edition   Second Edition   Third Edition   20th Anniversary Edition
May 2000   September 2002   August 2012   March 2020

XVII

PREFACE TO THE THIRD EDITION, 2012

Huge strides have been made in the hunt for alien life since the first edition of the book was published in 2000. None has been more significant than the launch of NASA's Kepler observatory in 2009. In three years, Kepler has discovered 61 new confirmed planets, including two Earth-like candidates and uncovered the possible existence of 2,300 more.

On the 26th December 2004 an undersea earthquake occurred, recorded at 9.1 on the Richter scale, just north of Simeulue Island, off the western coast of northern Sumatra, Indonesia. The earthquake triggered a series of devastating tsunamis that spread throughout the Indian Ocean, killing large numbers of people and inundating coastal communities across South and Southeast Asia, including parts of Indonesia, Sri Lanka, India and Thailand. The furthest recorded death due to the tsunami occurred some 8,000 km (5,000 miles) from the epicentre.

This earthquake was also reported to be the longest duration of faulting ever observed, lasting between 500 and 600 seconds, and it was large enough that it caused the entire planet to vibrate at least half an inch, or over a centimetre. It also triggered earthquakes in other locations as far away as Alaska.

This catastrophe is one of the deadliest disasters in modern history and highlights just how vulnerable our civilization is to natural events.

Is it possible a similar event occurred some 11,000 years ago, which devastated an ancient civilization which was thriving on our planet at this time? Are we the offspring of the survivors from this earlier catastrophic event as described in this book?

The English Heritage Conservation and Restoration Project 2007-2008 confirmed Silbury Hill is not simply a mound of chalk, a 'spoil heap', but was clinically constructed to a pre-determined complex plan. Can a conceivable ex-planation for the purpose of Silbury Hill be found by studying the most ancient and mysterious monuments found on Earth – pyramids. From the famous ancient pyramids in Egypt to the many newly discovered pyramids from Bosnia to China. The explorations of Pyramids, which are found on every continent on Earth, are examined in this latest edition. Why were hundreds if not thousands of pyramids built on every continent during our pre-history? It seems that pyramid geometry and their amazing scientific properties were clearly understood by our ancient ancestors?

Other sources of clues to our amazing evolution, including the emerging science of epigenetics, are also included in this third edition. Epigenetics provides an intriguing insight into how we may be able to re-discover our history in much greater detail than had hitherto seemed possible and confirm our extra-terrestrial heritage.

This edition of the book incorporates some of the excellent feedback received from emails, at lectures and via the website www.silburydawming.com.

PREFACE TO THE SECOND EDITION, 2002

The second edition expands on the *Alien Visitor* Gene Theory from feedback received since the book was first published in May 2000.

Hardly a day goes by without my attention being drawn to some new discovery which provides further evidence to the presence of an *Alien Visitor* on our planet or narrows the window of time when the *Alien Visitor* arrived and thrived on Earth.

For example, the 'Chilbolton Code' and 'Chilbolton Face' crop formations that appeared in August 2001, lend support to my belief that the *Alien Visitor* was able to transmit and receive messages both inside and outside Earth some 13,000 years ago. These signals have remained in the ether but could the 'messages' mysteriously appearing in crop fields close to some of the ancient monuments around the world, which I believe were built for the purpose of communications, also offer us clues to the existence of the *Alien Visitor* on Earth?

The section on our individuality in the chapter *It's All in the Mind* has been developed to explain how our alien knowledge has been inherited and reside in our individual trans-generation unconscious memory along with information from when life began up until the moment our life began. This inherited 'Operating System' defines our background, culture and religion and is open to manipulation. It can also explain reincarnation, superstitions, phobias, ghosts, poltergeists, UFOs and other supernatural and paranormal phenomena.

The subject 'imagination' has been separated from this chapter *It's All in the Mind* to its own chapter *Imagination*.

This edition of the book also incorporated some excellent feedback received via the website www.silburydawning.com which has been used to expand on some of the points made in the original book.

EPILOGUE TO THE THIRD EDITION, 2012

If we can image ourselves marooned on a remote planet, where although we are familiar with the *computer*, the *world wide web* and the *human genome*, it would be impossible to rebuild the technology in our lifetime. It would take some considerable time to develop the knowledge we had brought with us in the new world situation. Nevertheless, we would be able to use some of our practical skills to build a complex to enable us and our offspring to survive in this alien environment. However, if our civilisation failed through disease or a natural event, then the enduring parts of the complex we had built would look totally out of place on the planet when centuries later the civilisation was explored by our surviving offspring.

I believe this scenario has already occurred with the arrival of an extra-terrestrial or extra-terrestrials who were marooned on Earth some 13,000 years ago. We have inherited its immense knowledge via a trans-generational memory gene and we are slowly recovering our extra-terrestrial ancestor's knowledge. It would seem that although its time on Earth was relatively short, due to a natural disaster, they were able to use some of their practical knowledge to build sophisticated devices to help them adapt and survive in this new environment.

Are there any strange objects that look out-of-place on our landscape? Can our discoveries and futuristic predictions shed some light on the purpose of these mysterious constructions – the pyramids, Silbury Hill perhaps?

Around Silbury Hill, the use of materials such as sarsen stone and water combined with ley lines seems to indicate knowledge of energy. Were our alien ancestors able to generate electricity and produce powerful magnetic fields that could combat the force of gravity? This could explain the mythical tales of levitation and the ability of these ancients to construct Stonehenge and the Great Pyramid? Also, the ability to see the landscape from above – to fly!

Or have we yet to uncover the knowledge to understand the true purpose of these amazing ancient creations?

Today the cross pollination of the computer, biotech and quantum revolutions has released a tidal wave of discovery which has accelerated into the twenty first century. Our progress has gathered speed more in the past 50 years than in all of human history!

Futurists are already proclaiming areas which were quite recently seen as science fiction will become science fact in this century. Examples include 'supercomputers' that will enable us to reveal the secrets of everything; 'nuclear fusion' to preserve our fossil fuels and give us the ability to control global warming; 'space elevators' that will allow us to leapfrog the gravity barrier and allow us to explore space more cheaply; 'carbon nano tubes' even at the thickness of a human hair is one of the strongest materials known to man, 'nano bods' watchdogs that patrol our bodies looking for any signs of disease or decay; 'personal fabricators' that will give us the ability to create something out of nothing using nano technology; 'invisibility' (as per Harry Potter and previously from mythological tales via Plato) initially for military stealth purposes; 'teleportation' (from Star Trek's 'beam me up Scotty') has already been demonstrated at the photon level; 'artificial intelligence' that exceeds the bumbling human kind; 'intelligent robots' that will take us to Mars and beyond - to name but a few!

Are we slowly recovering this alien knowledge which has begun to accelerate over the past 50 years? So, will we reach the level of knowledge which was on our planet some 13,000 years ago? I believe we will!

SELECTED BIBLIOGRAPHY

Barnes, Michael   *Secrets of Lost Empires*   BBC Books 1996
Barrie, James M.   *The Admirable Crichton*   Sangam Books 1988
Bauval, Robert & Hancock, Graham   *Keeper of Genesis*   Mandarin 1997
Bennett, J.G.   *Deeper Man*   Turnstone Books 1978
Brennan, Herbie   *The Atlantis Enigma*   Piatkus 1999
Brian, Denis   *Einstein a Life*   John Wiley & Sons Ltd 1996
Buzan Tony   *The Mind Map Book*   BBC Books 1993

Campbell, Jonathan   *Deciphering the Dead Sea Scrolls*   Fontana Press 1996
Clarke, Sir Arthur C.   *2001: A Space Odyssey*   Legend 1990
Clavell, James   *King Rat*   Coronet 1975
Cohn, Norman   *Noah's Flood*   Yale University Press 1996
Cole, K.C.   *The Universe and the Teacup*   Little, Brown and Co (UK) 1998

Darwin, Charles   *The Origin of Species*   Penguin 1985
Defoe, Daniel   *Robinson Crusoe*   Oxford University Press 1972
Dennett, Daniel C.   *Darwin's Dangerous Idea*   Allen Lane 1995
Drosnin, Michael   *The Bible Code*   Orion 1997

Emery, W.B.   *Archaic Egypt*   Penguin Books 1991
Engel, Joel   *Gene Roddenberry*   Virgin Publishing 1994

Frankl, Viktor E.   *Man's Search for Meaning*   Beacon Press Boston 1959, 1962, 1984,1992
Frost Jr., S.E.   *Basic Teachings of the Great Philosophers*   Bantam Doubleday 1962

Gall, Edward   *The Mystery of Satan*   Printed by Reg Sharpe 1973
Gilbert, Adrian G.   *MAGI The Quest for a Secret Tradition*   Bloomsbury 1996
Golb, Norman   *Who Wrote the Dead Sea Scrolls?*   Michael O'Mara 1995
Golding, William   *Lord of the Flies*   Faber and Faber 1959
Gray, John   *Men are from Mars, Women are from Venus*   Thorsons 1999

Hancock, Graham   *Quest for the Lost Civilisation*   Penguin Books 1999   *Underworld*   Michael Joseph 2002
Hawking, Stephen W.   *A Brief History of Time*   Bantam Press 1990
Hope, Murry   *The Sirius Connection*   Element Books 1997
Huxley, Aldous   *Brave New World*   Grafton Books 1977

James, Alan   *Inner Tranquillity*   Aukana Trust 2002

Kaku, Michio   *Visions*   Oxford University Press 1998
Knight, Chris & Lomas, Robert   *The Hiram Key*   Arrow Books 1997

Leary Jim   *The Story of Silbury Hill*   English Heritage 2010
Lemesurier, Peter   *The Great Pyramid Decoded*   Element Books 1997

Mann, A.T.   *Millennium Prophecies*   Element Books 1992
Meaden, Terence   *The Circles Effect and Its Mysteries*   Artetech 1989
Morris, Desmond   *The Human Animal*   BBC Books 1994
Morris, Desmond   *The Naked Ape*   Vintage 1994

Noyes, Ralph   *The Crop Circle Enigma*   Gateway Books 1991

Oppenheimer, Professor Stephen *Out of Eden: The Peopling of the World* and *The Origins of the British: A Genetic Detective Story* Constable and Robinson 2004, 2007.
Ouspensky, P.D. *In Search of the Miraculous* Routledge 1957
Ovason, David *The Secrets of Nostradamus* Century Books 1997
Philips, Graham *Act of God* Pan Books 1998
Pierpaoli, Walter & Regelson, William *The Melatonin Miracle* Fourth Estate 1996
Pinker, Steven *How the Mind Works* Allen Lane 1997
Pitts, Mike *Hengeworld* Arrow Books 2000
Pond, Ray *The World's Religions* A Lion Handbook 1994
Porter, Roy *The Greatest Benefit to Mankind* Harper Collins 1997
Pringle, Lucy *Crop Circles The Greatest Mystery of Modern Times* Thorsons 1999

Ryan, Dr Bill & Pitman, Dr Walter *Noah's Flood* Simon & Schuster 1999

Schwaller de Lubicz, R.A. *Sacred Science* Inner Traditions International 1988
Shakespeare, William *The Tempest* Routledge 1988
Spencer, A.J. *Early Egypt* British Museum Press 1993

The Zanvyl Kreiger Mind/Brain Institute: Biennial Report 1993/1994
Thomas, Hugh *The Slave Trade: The History of the Atlantic Slave Trade, 1440-1870*   Macmillan 1998

Underwood, Guy *The Pattern of the Past* Museum Press 1968

West, John Anthony *Serpent in the Sky: The High Wisdom of Ancient Egypt* Quest Books 1993
Wilkinson, Jill D. & Campbell, Elizabeth *Psychology in Counselling and Therapeutic Practice* John Wiley and Sons 1997
Wilson, Elisabeth & Lewith, George *Natural Born Healers* Collins and Brown 1997
Wyeth Romy *The Stonehenge Story* Gemini 1998

With thanks to Element Books Ltd of Shaftesbury, Dorset; Little Brown and Co (UK), London; Random House Inc., New York, and Beacon Press, Boston for their permission to use extracts from their publications in *Silbury Dawning*.

INDEX

A

B

C

G

H

I

J

K

L

M

N

O

P

Q

R

S

T

U

V

W

Y

Z

Afterlife – My Eulogy

There is no Afterlife.

Seems cruel to deny those who have tragically or suddenly lost a loved one the solace of an Afterlife. So be it.

But had I known earlier in life that there was no Afterlife would I have been more: -

Loving and caring – *I believe I would.*

Kind and generous – *I believe I would.*

Mindful and willing to listen and learn from others – *I believe I would.*

Restrained with my obsessions – *I believe I would.*

Conscious of the world's wonders around me – *I believe I would.*

Appreciative and respectful of my Parents – *I wish I had.*

Aware of maintaining friendships through the highs and lows of life's' journey – *I wish I had.*

Involved in the pleasures and pastimes of the ones I love – *I wish I had.*

Time now seems strange. I can hear this eulogy being read out-loud and can see all the listening faces, although I won't be there.

But I WILL be there with you.

I will always be with you. Cherished memories, an unguarded reflection in a shop window.

I will be with you until the day you die.

There is no Afterlife.

No Heaven or Hell

Lightness or darkness.

No re-life.

No regrets, just profound relief after a fond farewell.

With all my love,

John

XLI

Printed in Great Britain
by Amazon